River Runners' Guide to Utah And Adjacent Areas

by

Gary Nichols

with illustrations by

Kirk Nichols

University of Utah Press
Salt Lake City
1986

Library of Congress Cataloging-in-Publication Data

Nichols, Gary C.
  River runners' guide to Utah and adjacent areas

  Rev. ed. of: River runners' guide to Utah. 1982.
  1. Canoes and canoeing—Utah—Guide-books.
  2. Rafting (Sports)—Utah—Guide-books. 3. Utah—
  Description and travel—1981-   —Guide-books.
  I. Nichols, Gary C. River runners' guide to Utah.
  II. Title.
  GV776.U8N52 1986   917.92   86-1688
  ISBN 0-87480-254-7

Cover: Kirk Nichols squeezes between rocks in one of many drops in the lower Black Box of the San Rafael River. Gary Nichols.

Back cover: The dynamic challenges of white water bring the author back time and again to the rivers. John Armstrong.

Contents

iv

1. Snake River
2. Bruneau River
3. Jarbidge River
4. Bear River—Black Canyon
5. Oneida Narrows
6. Logan River
7. Blacksmith Fork
8. Ogden River
9. South Fork of Ogden River
10. East Canyon Creek
11. Chalk Creek
12. Weber River
13. Bear River
14. Hayden Fork
15. East Fork of the Bear River
16. West Fork of Black's Fork
17. East Fork of Black's Fork
18. Big Cottonwood Creek
19. Little Cottonwood Creek
20. Surplus Canal
21. Jordan River
22. Provo River
23. Spanish Fork River
24. Strawberry River
25. Currant Creek
26. North Fork of the Duchesne River
27. Duchesne River
28. Rock Creek
29. Lake Fork
30. Yellowstone River
31. Uinta River
32. Green River—Red Canyon
33. Lodore Canyon
34. Yampa River
35. Split Mountain Canyon
36. White River
37. Desolation Canyon
38. Price River
39. San Rafael River
40. Huntington Creek
41. Cottonwood Creek
42. Ferron Creek
43. Labyrinth Canyon
44. Horsethief and Ruby Canyon
45. Westwater Canyon
46. Dolores River
47. Moab "Daily"
48. Gunnison River Gorge
49. Cataract Canyon
50. Dirty Devil River
51. Fremont River
52. Muddy Creek
53. Escalante River
54. San Juan River
55. Grand Canyon
56. Sevier River
57. Clear Creek
58. Salina Creek
59. North Fork of the Virgin River
60. Virgin River

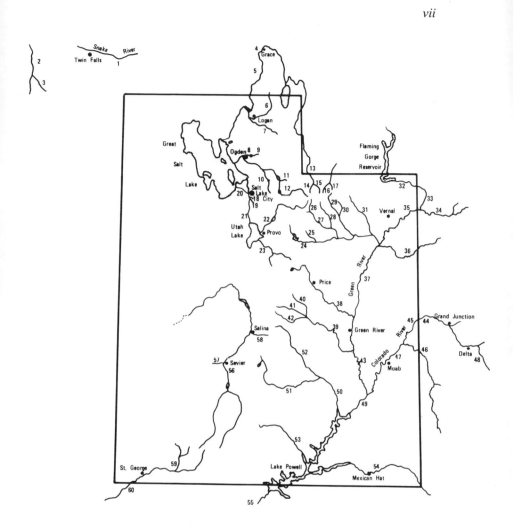

Caution

River running can be extremely dangerous, and no one should under-
take to run any river without receiving proper instruction from a
qualified person or organization. Degrees of difficulty are at best subjec-
tive assessments, and conditions can alter with changes in water level,
seasons of the year, equipment used, and experience of the river runner.
Natural and human events can radically alter statements made about
various runs, and craft and equipment must be selected in terms of the
difficulty of the run and experience of the user in order to assure the
utmost safety. River runners are reminded that current information
about particular river trips can only be obtained by contacting the
sources mentioned in the text to determine the latest river conditions
prior to embarking on a run. While not all rivers discussed were field
checked by the author, most were, and experienced river runners and
other reliable sources were consulted to gain accurate information. *The
user of this book, not the publisher or author, assumes full responsibility for maintaining personal safety when running the rivers discussed in
the text or using other information discussed in the text.*

Shake Fork

Acknowledgments

There are many people who, both knowingly and unknowingly, played some part in the creation of this book. Thanks to all of them, especially the following: My wife, Jeanette, for her never-ending encouragement, for driving shuttle and waiting up to 5 hours when I misjudged the time, and for letting me go for days at a time to fulfill my urge to explore; my brother Kirk for teaching me to kayak, for accompanying me on many trips, for filling in some descriptions with information I wasn't aware of, and for his many drawings and photographs; Lane Johnson for being the main force to get me to write a river guide, for going with me on many exploratory trips, and for his editorial help and photos; Brian Smoot for his help in doing the maps, along with the University of Utah Geography Department for use of their equipment; Peter Hovingh, who was accidently left out of the first edition, for his guidance to the White River and his river preservation efforts; the American Whitewater Affiliation for allowing me to reprint their *Safety Code;* and the USGS for access to their water data and maps. Thanks to others who accompanied me on exploratory trips: Bob Cooper, Richard Floisand, Ed Gertler, Dave Hildebrand, and Neil Kahn. Thanks to Cal Giddings and Les Jones for their information on the many rivers they explored. Special thanks to all those who take care of the rivers they use.

Introduction

Utah has some truly impressive rivers. Most are small, some are power-
ful and muddy, others are quiet and scenic, many offer thrills and spills.
Running those rivers on a raft, kayak or a canoe offers a unique way to
experience nature. Whatever the level of challenge or type of scenery
you seek, it is available on Utah's rivers.

The huge runoff of 1983 and 1984 has changed many of the rivers
described in the first edition of *River Runners' Guide to Utah*. The high
water during those years made river running possible in many smaller
streams, some of which rival or surpass the best rivers described in the
first edition. With new challenges opened up and several descriptions
needing revision, I decided it was time to update and expand this book.

Since the publication of the first edition, the Virgin River between
Virgin and La Verkin in southwestern Utah has been lost to the Quail
Creek Project. The river is now buried in a pipeline and the deep, beautiful canyon has been desecrated by construction. The many animals
and birds, including some bald eagles, will have to move elsewhere to
find the life-giving water that has been stolen from them. A couple of
men are richer, the rest of us are poorer. Hopefully, revising this guide
will make more people aware of the variety of rivers found in Utah so
that, through awareness, we can work to preserve them. Maybe future
development projects will not slip by as unnoticed as this one did.

A few rivers outside of Utah have been added to this edition. These
are some of the region's more scenic and challenging runs. While most
are rivers that flow into or out of Utah, those few that don't are rivers as
accessible to Utah river runners as they are to boaters in states bordering
Utah.

Maps have been included to show a general picture of the area and
the shuttle roads leading to the river considered. A small insert of Utah
is on each map with a shaded area showing the location of the river
segment. A Utah road map, in addition, will provide a good overall
view of where the rivers are and how to get to them. For exacting detail,
refer to the United States Geological Survey (USGS) topographical
maps listed at the beginning of each section.

The rivers are listed alphabetically for ease of reference if you already know their names. If you are going to a certain area of Utah and
want to know what rivers are near there, look at the Utah map at the
beginning of the book to find the names of the rivers and then look up
the description. An appendix to this book lists the rivers according to
difficulty. For example, if you are just interested in intermediate runs
you can look there to find them without having to go through the description of every river.

This book may appear biased toward kayakers and probably is, in spite of attempts not to be. I do more kayaking than other types of river running; however, I've run up to Class 4 rapids in canoes and rafts and have had some river experience with inflatable kayaks, sportyaks, inner tubes, and boogie boards, so I am aware of what can and can't be done in a variety of craft. (I'm not recommending inner tubes or boogie boards on most rivers. Many people who use them are not experienced enough and not properly equipped with helmet, wetsuit, and lifejacket.) The nature of Utah's rivers themselves biases this book. Once you get away from the major rivers a preponderance of what's left is more suitable to small craft, particularly a kayak, C-1 or C-2 (one- and two-person decked canoes). Rafts are just too big for many of Utah's streams.

There aren't any "Craft" headings beginning each section as in the first edition of this book. The type of craft that can be taken down a stretch of river depends on the ability of the person controlling it. You should know your river-running ability better than I do. If you don't, then consider yourself a beginner. Generally speaking, however, decked boaters (kayaks, C-1's, and C-2's) with enough skill are the only ones who should be attempting small, rocky, high-gradient rivers. Quite a few of the rivers listed in this book fit into this category. Rafters and open canoeists should generally avoid these and streams with log-jam problems, since they may not be able to maneuver or stop quickly enough to avoid the logs. I realize that some rafters and open canoeists are safely running these types of rivers with up to Class 5 rapids. That's why I'm not telling you what type of craft to use, but you should be aware that these are people with an extremely high skill level who have taken every safety precaution and used specialized equipment such as self-bailing rafts and royalex canoes filled with flotation. Several deaths show the price you might pay for a mistake.

To get an idea of whether you and your craft can make it down a stretch of river, look at the DIFFICULTY heading with each section, read the description, and consider the following general guidelines. If you've never taken your craft on any type of water, get some instruction before trying even a beginner run. Universities, local clubs, Red Cross chapters, and stores selling river-running equipment often offer classes. If you've never been on anything but lakes, no matter how skilled, consider yourself a beginning river runner. Whatever your craft, you should gradually work up from beginner runs so that you can learn what your ability level is and get a feel for the ratings in this book.

In this guide, each river description starts out with a summary of basic information you need to know to determine when, where, and how to run the river. The following is an explanation of how to use these headings.

Difficulty: The ratings used in this edition are based on the International

Scale of River Difficulty, rating rapids from Class 1 (the easiest) to Class 6 (the most difficult). Several possible ways of changing this scale to make it more accurate and allow for addition of more difficult runs have been proposed. Hopefully, the bugs will be worked out of these soon. Until then these ratings give you a rough idea of what to expect. They are not exact. A Class 4 rapid to me might be a Class 3+ to you or a Class 5− to someone else. Also, keep in mind that ratings may change as the river flow goes up or down. Along with this difficulty rating I've listed specific types of hazards to expect. This will help you know why it received the rating it has. I've also noted when I think a raft would have trouble. But the final decision about whether to run a rapid or portage is yours to make after scouting the section and assessing your ability.

INTERNATIONAL SCALE OF RIVER DIFFICULTY

If rapids on a river generally fit into one of the following classifications, but the water temperature is below 50 degrees F., or if the trip is an extended one in a wilderness area, the river should be considered one class more difficult than normal.

Class 1. Moving water with a few riffles and small waves. Few or no obstructions.

Class 2. Easy rapids with waves up to three feet, and wide, clear channels that are obvious without scouting. Some maneuvering is required.

Class 3. Rapids with high, irregular waves often capable of swamping an open canoe. Narrow passages that often require complex maneuvering. May require scouting from shore.

Class 4. Long, difficult rapids with constricted passages that often require precise maneuvering in very turbulent waters. Scouting from shore is often necessary, and conditions make rescue difficult. Generally not possible for open canoes. Boaters in covered canoes and kayaks should be able to Eskimo roll.

Class 5. Extremely difficult, long, and very violent rapids with highly congested routes which nearly always must be scouted from shore. Rescue conditions are difficult and there is significant hazard to life in event of a mishap. Ability to Eskimo roll is essential for kayaks and canoes.

Class 6. Difficulties of Class 5 carried to the extreme of navigability. Nearly impossible and very dangerous. For teams of experts only, after close study and with all precautions taken.

Length: Sometimes I've included times along with actual distances. Generally speaking you can go about 15 to 20 miles per day in a raft and 20 or more in a canoe or kayak. Many variables can affect this, including wind, water speed, your physical condition, craft design, and the difficulty of the river. I've averaged as little as 1 mile per hour on rivers where I've had to do a lot of scouting and portaging.

Time of Year: This will list the most likely time of year to find reasonable levels for river running. Some rivers are runnable year-round. Others have very short seasons that are difficult to predict. The National Weather Service can give you a general idea of the water situation for a given area and let you know when they expect a river to peak.

Average Gradient: This lists the drop of the river in feet per mile. Rivers rarely have a smooth steady gradient, so expect a river to have sections dropping both more and less than the average. Generally, the higher the gradient the more difficult the river; however, this is greatly affected by the volume of water and whether there are obstacles in the river. Don't be fooled by one that's flat at the put-in and flat at the take-out. These are often flat and why they are good access points. Check the average gradient to see what you can expect through the rest of the section.

Flow Levels: This lists the normal high and the record high. The normal high does not include flash floods that briefly can bring the river to many times its normal high. It's based on runoff highs that usually last many days. The record high includes the highest known flow under any condition, often happening when flash flooding occurs simultaneously with spring runoff. It also often happens in August or September when we get most of our thunderstorms. Flows are listed in cubic feet per second (cfs). This is figured by taking the average depth at a given spot on the river, times the width, times the distance in feet the water moves in one second. So a river 50 feet wide with an average depth of 2 feet, flowing at the speed of 4 feet per second would have a flow level of $2 \times 50 \times 4 = 400$ cfs. For flow information on the more common runs call the River Recreational Report in Salt Lake City: (801) 539-1311. A recording provided by the National Weather Service gives that morning's readings plus a forecast of both flow and weather. For personal help from them their Salt Lake City number is (801) 524-5130.

Topo Maps: These are maps put out by the U.S. Geological Survey (USGS) that show contour lines. Most listed are the 7.5 minute series, a scale of 1 to 24,000, and show great detail of roads, trails, and topography. You can figure out the gradients of rivers from these and tell whether the river is going through a narrow canyon or through flat open country. Side canyons and every bend in the river are shown so they can be used to keep track of exactly where you are as you go down a river.

Access: This tells you what roads to use to get to and from the river. This will make the most sense if used in conjunction with the maps in the book.

First Run: After my first guidebook, several people suggested that it would be interesting to know who made the first run down a river, so

I've included those I could find. I don't know any way to contact everyone who might possibly have been the first except to publish a list and let people call me to make necessary corrections. I've contacted many people, especially those I know have been running rivers for a long time, and have listed the information obtained. I think most of this is correct; however, if you ran one of these rivers or know someone who did previous to the date listed, please call and let me know. I apologize if you've been left out and will correct it in future editions. Call or write Gary Nichols, 3495 West 8245 South, West Jordan, Utah 84084; phone (801) 255-2295.

SAFETY

When using this guide or any other, be aware that rivers change and that varying flow levels create great differences. You can only count on a guidebook to be accurate in a general way. For this reason, we do not assume responsibility for inaccuracies or omissions.

Learn all you can about any river you're considering running so that you'll know if it's within your ability. That's one of the purposes of this guide—to help you know what to plan for. Know where the closest help will be. Be prepared to hike out if necessary. Take plenty of drinking water. There are almost no rivers in Utah that are drinkable without treating. Even if the water looks clean and is high in the mountains it probably has a microscopic organism called *Giardia lamblia* that will make you sick a week or two later. Don't take a chance; boil it or purify it in some other reliable way.

I highly recommend that you get advanced first-aid training, especially if you're planning trips away from roads and civilization. Understand hypothermia, mouth-to-mouth resuscitation, how to stop severe bleeding, and how to treat broken bones. Throughout much of Utah you'll find rattlesnakes, black widow spiders, and scorpions. Know what to do should you be stung or bitten.

Learn the basic skills of boating well and stay within your ability. Classes are best for learning the basics. If you're kayaking in difficult water, a reliable Eskimo roll on both sides is important. In most cases, you're far safer in your boat than swimming alongside it.

It's also important to know how to rescue yourself and others. A quick rescue will often prevent equipment loss and much more serious situations such as injuries and hypothermia. Don't expect to handle a situation properly if all you've done is read about what to do. Read all you can, but also practice before the need arises. The University of Utah offers a river safety and rescue class; an excellent book is *River Rescue* by Les Bechdel and Slim Ray.

Be sure you have adequate flotation—in the boat and on yourself. Most canoes need extra flotation when used on a river. Rafts should have at least 3 separate air chambers, preferably 4. Wear life jackets and have them strapped on tight enough that they won't be pulled off by turbulent water.

The American Whitewater Affiliation (AWA) publishes an excellent safety code which is reproduced at the end of the introduction. For additional copies of the AWA Safety Code, send a stamped, self-addressed envelope to: AWA Safety Code, 146 N. Brockway, Palatine, Illinois 60067.

WILDERNESS ETIQUETTE

One of the nicest aspects about river running is traveling through wilderness areas without leaving a trace. Unfortunately some river runners don't seem to care what they do to the environment or what kind of reputation they give everyone else. Desert environments are especially fragile. Decomposition is slow and it is much harder for plants to grow back after being damaged. Let me suggest some guidelines for wilderness etiquette.

1. Carry out all refuse, including grease from cooking.
2. Carry out all human waste. This isn't necessary in uncrowded areas if people bury their own waste 4 to 6 inches deep, well away from the river, and either carry out or burn toilet paper.
3. Do not use soap—even biodegradable soap—directly in the river. Wash and rinse well above the high-water mark.
4. Use a stove for cooking or carry a fire pan. If you must build a fire, build only one per group and only when really needed.
5. Use only downed wood for fires. Do not cut standing trees, alive or dead, and never strip off limbs or bark.
6. Carry your ashes out with you or scatter them in the swift part of the river in areas where this is allowed.
7. Respect private property. Much of the land along the rivers is privately owned. The few owners I have met have been quite friendly, but this could change if one person damages property, litters, or otherwise creates a nuisance. Get permission if you must cross private property.
8. When passing other groups, respect their right to enjoy the wilderness in peace and quiet.
9. When passing fishermen, respect their rights to the river. Some who haven't caught anything all day may think you have just ruined their chances, so the best policy is to stay as far away as possible. By giving them a wide berth you may avoid having rocks thrown at you as has happened to me. Most fishermen are friendly and often curious about river running. Remember that they are natural allies in the fight for river preservation.

10. Be aware of antiquities laws. Do not destroy or remove anything from any ruins you find. There are many extremely interesting ruins, pictographs, and petroglyphs near some of Utah's rivers. Leave them alone for others to enjoy.

RIVER ORGANIZATIONS

Whether you are a canoeist, rafter, kayaker, sportyaker, inner tuber, or just a curious spectator, you have an interest in maintaining and improving river environments. There are several local and national organizations of river runners and conservation groups who support river sports and organize efforts aimed at protecting our rivers from pollution and damaging encroachment. You may well want to get involved. The following are some of the better-known national organizations:

ACA   American Canoe Association
       P.O. Box 10748
       Des Moines, Iowa 50349
       Publication: CANOE Magazine

ARCC American Rivers Conservation Council
       323 Pennsylvania Avenue SE
       Washington, D.C. 20003

AWA   American Whitewater Affiliation
       146 North Brockway
       Palatine, Illinois 60067
       Publication: AMERICAN WHITEWATER JOURNAL

NORS National Organization for River Sports
       P.O. Box 6847
       Colorado Springs, Colorado 80934
       Publication: CURRENTS Magazine

An excellent magazine (not published by a river organization) is:

       RIVER RUNNER
       P.O. Box 2047
       Vista, California 92083

Safety Code

American Whitewater Affiliation

A guide to safe river boating in canoe, kayak or raft. Prepared and published by the **American Whitewater Affiliation,** a volunteer organization of paddlers and clubs interested in whitewater sport, and publishers of the bimonthly *American Whitewater Journal,* which offers not only entertainment but also up-to-date information on technique, equipment, safety, conservation, racing and river access developments as well as a complete listing of affiliated clubs and how to contact them.

I. PERSONAL PREPAREDNESS AND RESPONSIBILITY

1. **Be a Competent Swimmer** with ability to handle yourself underwater.

2. **WEAR a Lifejacket.**

3. **Keep Your Craft Under Control.** Control must be good enough at all times to stop or reach shore before you reach any danger. Do not enter a rapid unless you are reasonably sure you can safely navigate it or swim the entire rapid in event of capsize.

4. **BE AWARE OF RIVER HAZARDS AND AVOID THEM. Following are the most frequent KILLERS.**

    A. **HIGH WATER.** The river's power and danger, and the difficulty of rescue, increase tremendously as the flow rate increases. It is often misleading to judge river level at the put-in. Look at a narrow, critical passage. Could a *sudden* rise from sun on a snow pack, rain, or a dam release occur on your trip?

    B. **COLD.** Cold quickly robs one's strength, along with one's will and ability to save oneself. Dress to protect yourself from cold water and weather extremes. When the water temperature is less than 50 degrees F., a diver's wetsuit is essential for safety in event of an upset. Next best is wool clothing under a windproof outer garment such as a splash-proof nylon shell; in this case one should also carry matches and a complete change of clothes in a waterproof package. If, after prolonged exposure, a person experiences uncontrollable shaking or has difficulty talking and moving, he must be warmed immediately by whatever means available.

C. **STRAINERS.** Brush, fallen trees, bridge pilings, or anything else which allows river current to sweep through but pins boat and boater against the obstacle. The water pressure on anything trapped this way is overwhelming, and there may be little or no whitewater to warn of danger.

D. **WEIRS, REVERSALS, AND SOUSE HOLES.** The water drops over an obstacle, then curls back on itself in a stationary wave, as is often seen at weirs and dams. The surface water is actually going UPSTREAM, and this action will trap any floating object between the drop and the wave. Once trapped, a swimmer's only hope is to dive below the surface where current is flowing downstream, or try to swim out the end of the wave.

5. **Boating Alone** is not recommended. The preferred minimum is three craft.

6. **Have a Frank Knowledge of Your Boating Ability.** Don't attempt waters beyond this ability. Learn paddling skills and teamwork, if in a multiple-manned craft, to match the river you plan to boat.

7. **Be in Good Physical Condition** consistent with the difficulties that may be expected.

8. **Be Practiced in Escape** from an overturned craft, in self rescue, in rescue, and in **Artificial Respiration.** Know first aid.

9. **The Eskimo Roll** should be mastered by kayakers and canoers planning to run large rivers and/or rivers with continuous rapids where a swimmer would have trouble reaching shore.

10. **Wear a Crash Helmet** where an upset is likely. This is essential in a kayak or covered canoe.

11. **Be Suitably Equipped.** Wear shoes that will protect your feet during a bad swim or a walk for help, yet will not inter-

fere with swimming (tennis shoes recommended). Carry a knife and waterproof matches. If you need eyeglasses, tie them on and carry a spare pair. Do not wear bulky clothing that will interfere with your swimming when water-logged.

II. BOAT AND EQUIPMENT PREPAREDNESS

1. **Test New and Unfamiliar Equipment** before relying on it for difficult runs.

2. **Be Sure Craft is in Good Repair** before starting a trip. Eliminate sharp projections that could cause injury during a swim.

3. Inflatable craft should have **Multiple Air Chambers** and should be test inflated before starting a trip.

4. **Have Strong, Adequately Sized Paddles or Oars** for controlling the craft and carry sufficient spares for the length of the trip.

5. **Install Flotation Devices** in non-inflatable craft, securely fixed, and designed to displace as much water from the craft as possible.

6. **Be Certain There is Absolutely Nothing to Cause Entanglement** when coming free from an upset craft; i.e., a spray skirt that won't release or tangles around legs; life jacket buckles or clothing that might snag; canoe seats that lock on shoe heels; foot braces that fail or allow feet to jam under them; flexible decks that collapse on boater's legs when a kayak is trapped by water pressure; baggage that dangles in an upset; loose rope in the craft, or badly secured bow/stern lines.

7. **Provide Ropes to Allow You to Hold Onto Your Craft** in case of upset, and so that it may be rescued. Following are the recommended methods:

   A. **Kayaks and Covered Canoes** should have 6 inch diameter grab loops of 1/4 inch rope attached to bow and stern. A stern painter 7 or 8 feet long is optional and may be used if properly secured to prevent entanglement.

   B. **Open Canoes** should have bow and stern lines (painters) securely attached consisting of 8 to 10 feet of 1/4 or 3/8 inch rope. These lines must be *secured* in such a way that they will not come loose accidentally and entangle the boaters during a swim, yet they must be ready for immediate use during an emergency. Attached balls, floats, and knots are *not* recommended.

   C. **Rafts and Dories** should have taut perimeter grab lines threaded through the loops usually provided.

8. **Respect Rules for Craft Capacity** and know how these capacities should be reduced for whitewater use. (Life raft ratings must generally be halved.)

9. **Carry Appropriate Repair Materials:** tape (heating duct tape) for short trips, complete repair kit for wilderness trips.

10. **Car Top Racks Must Be Strong** and positively attached to the vehicle, and each boat must be tied to each rack. In addition, each end of each boat should be tied to car bumper. Suction cup racks are poor. The entire arrangement should be able to withstand all but the most violent vehicle accident.

III. LEADER'S PREPAREDNESS AND RESPONSIBILITY

1. **River Conditions.** Have a reasonable knowledge of the difficult parts of the run, or if an exploratory trip, examine maps to estimate the feasibility of the run. Be aware of possible rapid changes in river level, and how these changes can affect the difficulty of the run. If important, determine approximate flow rate or level. If trip involves important tidal currents, secure tide information.

2. **Participants.** Inform participants of expected river conditions and determine if the prospective boaters are qualified for the trip. All decisions should be based on group safety and comfort. Difficult decisions on the participation of marginal boaters must be based on total group strength.

3. **Equipment.** Plan so that all necessary group equipment is present on the trip; 50 to 100 foot throwing rope, first aid kit with fresh and adequate supplies, extra paddles, repair materials, and survival equipment if appropriate. Check equipment as necessary at the put-in, especially: life jackets, boat flotation, and any items that could prevent complete escape from the boat in case of an upset.

4. **Organization.** Remind each member of individual responsibility in keeping group compact and intact between leader and sweep (capable rear boater). If group is too large, divide into smaller groups, each of appropriate boating strength, and designate group leaders and sweeps.

5. **Float Plan.** If trip is into a wilderness area, or for an extended period, your plans should be filed with appropriate authorities, or left with someone who will contact them after a certain time. Establishment of checkpoints along the way at which civilization could be contacted if necessary should be considered. Knowing location of possible help could speed rescue in any case.

IV. IN CASE OF UPSET

1. **Evacuate Your Boat Immediately** if there is imminent danger of being trapped against logs, brush, or any other form of strainer.

2. **Recover With an Eskimo Roll if Possible.**

3. **If You Swim, Hold Onto Your Craft.** It has much flotation and is easy for rescuers to spot. Get to the upstream end so craft cannot crush you against obstacles.

4. **Release Your Craft if This Improves Your Safety.** If rescue is not imminent and water is numbing cold, or if worse rapids follow, then strike out for the nearest shore.

5. **When Swimming Rocky Rapids,** use backstroke with legs downstream and **Feet Near the Surface.** If your foot wedges on the bottom, fast water will push you under and hold you there. **Get to Slow Or Very Shallow Water Before Trying to Stand or Walk. Look Ahead.** Avoid possible entrapment situations: rock wedges, fissures, strainers, brush, logs, weirs, reversals and souse holes. Watch for eddies and slackwater so that you can be ready to use these when you approach. Use every opportunity to work your way toward shore.

6. If others spill, **Go After the Boaters.** Rescue boats and equipment only if this can be done safely.

A New System of Universal River Signals*

STOP: Potential hazard ahead. Wait for "all clear" signal before proceeding, or scout ahead. Form a horizontal bar with your paddle or outstretched arms. Move up and down to attract attention, using a pumping motion with paddle or flying motion with arms. Those seeing the signal should pass it back to others in the party.

*Signaling system devised by AWA committee composed of Jim Sindelar, Tom McCloud, O.K. Goodwin, Bev Hartline, Walt Blackadar and Charles Walbridge. Illustrations by Les Fry.

HELP/EMERGENCY: Assist the signaller as quickly as possible. Give three long blasts on a police whistle while waving a paddle, helmet or life vest over your head in a circular motion. If a whistle is not available, use the visual signal alone. A whistle is best carried on a lanyard attached to the shoulder of a life vest.

ALL CLEAR: Come ahead (In the absence of other directions, proceed down the center.) Form a vertical bar with your paddle or one arm held high above your head. Paddle blade should be turned flat for maximum visibility. To signal direction or a preferred course through a rapid around obstruction, lower the previously vertical ''all clear'' by 45 degrees toward the side of the river with the preferred route. Never point toward the obstacle you wish to avoid.

The American Whitewater Safety Code, in lots of 50, is available at a low cost to cover printing and mailing: Write American Whitewater Affiliation, P.O. Box 1261, Jefferson City, MO 65102. Send self-addressed, stamped envelope for a single copy.

NORTH SLOPE UINTA MOUNTAINS

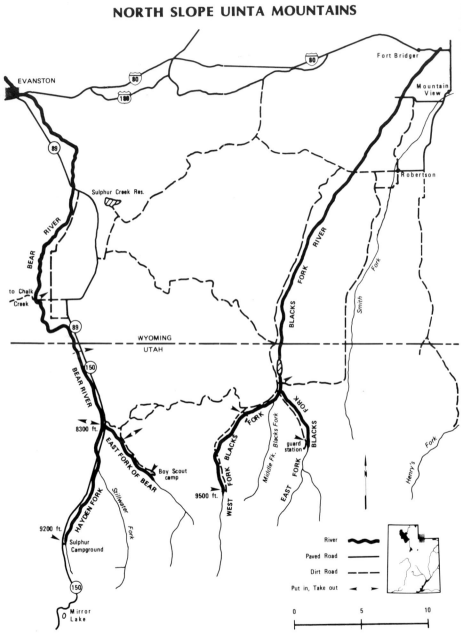

Bear River

EAST FORK, HAYDEN FORK, AND MAIN BEAR

Difficulty: Class 1 to 4. Steep, rocky, log jams, tight turns.
Length: Since roads generally follow each section, your run can be whatever length you want.
Time of Year: Late spring. The river usually peaks in early June.
Average Gradient: East Fork, 91 ft./mi. (bottom 2.5 miles is 125 ft./mi.); Hayden Fork, 82 ft./mi.; Bear River, 85 ft./mi.
Flow Levels: The gage on the East Fork is 4.1 miles above the mouth; the average peak is around 500 cfs, with a record of 631 cfs on 4 July 1975. The Bear River gage is 2.8 miles south of the Utah-Wyoming line; the average peak is about 2,000 cfs with a record of 2,980 cfs on 6 June 1968.
Topo Maps: Whitney Reservoir, Christmas Meadows, Deadman Mountain, Pine Knoll, Myers Reservoir.
Access: U-150 follows most of Hayden Fork and the Bear; the East Fork is accessible by dirt road.
First Run: East Fork—Les Jones, 15 July 1973, 31 May 1974; Hayden Fork—Les Jones, June 1956, 18 May 1974, 4 June 1974; Bear—Cal Giddings, Les Jones, Roger Turnes, 10 June 1972.

EAST FORK OF THE BEAR

The East Fork and the Hayden Fork join to form the Bear River. Just north of where they join (about 6 miles south of the Utah-Wyoming border), a dirt logging road leaves U-150, a right fork in the road cuts back to the East Fork, and generally follows the river to the East Fork of Bear Boy Scout camp. The fastest stretch (Class 3 to 4−) starts just upstream from where the road first comes to the river; above here the river is a little gentler but still not for beginners. A longer run could start at the scout camp, giving you a good idea of whether you can handle the rougher, 2.5-mile stretch to the confluence with the Hayden Fork.

Below the scout camp the river winds through meadows until you come to a gage. It then drops faster through a narrow canyon for about a half mile and then winds through more meadows until the last steep stretch. This last stretch, one of the steeper runnable sections of river in the Uintas, takes about 45 minutes to run (plus scouting time) and is shallow, fast, rocky, and often blocked in spots by logs.

HAYDEN FORK

If you want a peaceful float on a tiny river through willows and over beaver dams, the 4 miles from Sulphur Creek Campground on U-150 to where the willows end is nice. After this, the river becomes much steeper, rockier, and potentially dangerous because of logjams. Except for the upper flat section, this is mainly Class 2 to 3. It crosses under U-150 just below Stillwater Campground, which is about 5 miles below where the willows end or 9 miles from Sulphur Campground. It's another 3.5 miles to the confluence with the East Fork. The last mile is the steepest part.

BEAR RIVER

Two camping areas are located where the Hayden Fork and East Fork come together to form the Bear River. One is on Hayden Fork and is called the Bear River Campground. The other is just below the confluence and is called East Fork of the Bear Campground. You can camp at either and put in right from camp.

The river is good sized here compared to the two forks that form it. It's wider but still fairly shallow and rocky. The first 3 miles is best— constant Class 2 to 3 with almost no break. Then the river starts splitting into many small, swift channels, creating logjam danger.

Take out can be a problem since the land bordering the river is private property. About 5.5 miles from the put-in (a mile before the Wyoming border) is a bridge and a gage. A short walk takes you up to the highway through a gate. It's about 10 more miles to the bridge to Chalk Creek and then another 20 river miles to where the highway crosses the river.

BLACK CANYON AND ONEIDA NARROWS

Difficulty: Black Canyon, Class 3 to 5. Steep, rocky drops, holes. Would be extremely difficult for a raft. Oneida Narrows, Class 1 to 2+.

Length: Black Canyon, 7 miles; Oneida Narrows, 6 miles to ID-36, 5 miles more to ID-34.

Time of Year: Both sections are controlled by dams; usually highest in May and June.

Average Gradient: Black Canyon, 70 ft./mi.; Oneida Narrows, 20 ft./mi.

Flow Levels: The Black Canyon section used to be almost dry because 900 cfs is diverted through a pipe to the power plant. Since 1983 it has been runnable most of the time with flows from 800 to 2,500 cfs. I'm not sure if this is due strictly to the excess water or if there is some other reason as well. The Oneida Narrows section has a normal high of about 2,000 cfs with a record of 5,480 cfs on 8 May 1922. The gage is 200 feet downstream from the tailrace of the Oneida Power Plant. Call the Utah Power and Light hydrology department in Salt Lake City for flow information (801) 535-2174.

Topo Maps: Soda Springs, Bancroft, Riverdale.

Access: ID-34 and ID-36.

First Run: Black Canyon—Bryan Seeholzer, Graham Stork, Larry Dunn, and Cliff Stocks, 3 September 1983.

Reverse pop-ups are hard to avoid, as Lane Johnson finds out, when running the steep drops in Boo Boo Rapid in Black Canyon of the Bear River. Lane Johnson appears left of center. Gary Nichols.

BLACK CANYON

Most of this run is in a beautiful, 100-foot-deep canyon hidden in the middle of a valley. The first part of the canyon has sheer basalt walls. Turner Road (Main Street) going west out of Grace, Idaho, crosses this section and offers a tremendous view of the canyon and the waterfall section. Not long after this the basalt becomes broken and less sheer. It's still very beautiful although ominous looking with twisted juniper

BEAR RIVER - BLACK CANYON

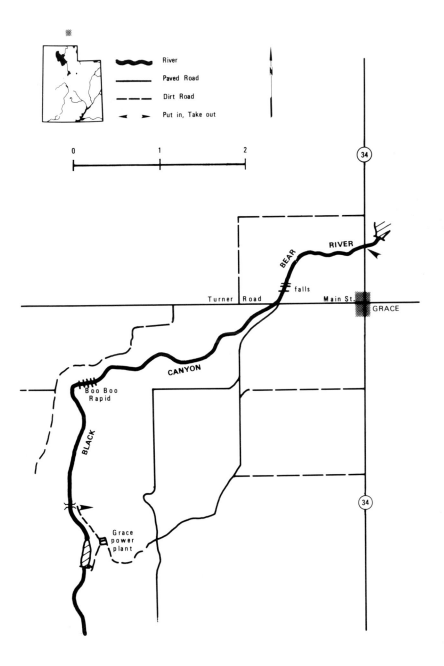

trees lurking above the jagged, dark rocks. Occasionally an area is marred by trash dumped over the canyon rim by residents.

From the put-in under the bridge at the north end of Grace, the river and countryside are flat for about a mile. After a Class 1 shallow area, the river cuts quickly into the basalt, creating a couple of Class 3 drops and then a large pool above a triple falls (Class 4+). Get out here and scout. The first two falls are shorter but somewhat tricky, then comes a short pool followed by a 12-foot falls. It has been run in a few different places. The pool below is deep and I've never seen it hold anyone at flows below 1,600 cfs. Above 2,000 cfs the falls can be dangerous.

Many Class 3 and 4 rapids follow this (most of them fairly narrow) as do some excellent surfing and endo spots. Be on the lookout for several holes that are both hard to see and hard to get out of, depending on flow. One rapid you come to spreads wider than the rest; take the left or you'll end up in a boulder field that has no route through.

About two-thirds of the way through the run you'll see some houses high up on the bluff ahead. A Class 3 rapid starts below a pool here. There's an eddy on the right at the end of this rapid just above a narrow, steep drop. Don't miss this eddy. The drop goes into a riverwide hole and is the beginning of the hardest rapid (Class 5), called Boo Boo. Scout this carefully and decide if and where you want to run it. It's long and rocky, and a number of nasty swims have taken place here, resulting in lost equipment and bruised bodies. A big pool is found at the end of the rapid.

The last couple of miles is full of short, steep boulder drops (Class 3 to 4) that are close together. Watch out for hidden holes. The river spreads out the last quarter mile above the take-out, which is on the left under a large footbridge.

ONEIDA NARROWS

This section is just a few miles north of Preston, Idaho. The description is at high water when it's most exciting. Lower water is slower and easier.

If you put in at the bridge below the dam, you have fast water for about a half mile and then it widens and slows for about a mile. The canyon narrows and several Class 1 and 2 rapids prove challenging for an open canoe in high water. The steepest part lasts about a mile.

About 4.5 miles from the dam is a steep drop all the way across the river. The right and left sides were runnable when I was there. A pipe runs across the river at the end of the canyon just before ID-36. Under it is a low dam, the right side of which was runnable.

After going under ID-36, it's about 4.5 miles to ID-34, with a good current, a few rocks, and some small rapids and a diversion along the way. ID-36 generally follows the river but is only right next to it in a few spots.

6

BIG & LITTLE COTTONWOOD CREEKS

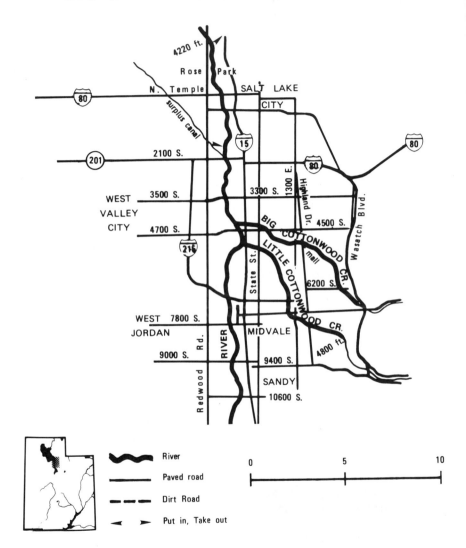

Big Cottonwood Creek

Difficulty: Class 1 to 4. Fast, rocky, small, several dams and low bridges, a few logs.
Length: 8.5 miles.
Time of Year: Late May to early June.
Average Gradient: 48 ft./mi. (first 3 miles is 93 ft./mi.)
Flow Levels: Normal high is 300 to 400 cfs with a record flow of 1,040 cfs on 26 September 1982.
Topo Maps: Sugar House, SLC South.
Access: Many city streets (not all shown on map).
First Run: Bob Cooper, Spring 1973.

Most people are familiar with the canyon section of this creek that cascades past picnic and camping areas. The 300+ ft./mi. drop makes boating here suicidal. However, after leaving the mouth of the canyon it begins to ease and becomes an exciting little urban stream that's boatable for a short time during the spring. It's best to run it before it peaks, especially in a high-water year, because the channel is usually cleaned to prepare for runoff. After the peak, it's often full of snags and other debris.

The section below the water treatment plant and above the catch pond could possibly be run at about 300 cfs if done right after it has been cleared and dredged—before the rocks are all washed back in by high flows. This section is extremely steep (250 ft./mi.) and it would be almost impossible to stop.

At high flows especially, the section from the catch pond by the Old Mill to 6200 South is very fast with big waves but very few eddies. This should probably all be scouted before starting.

After the first bridge below the catch pond is a drop that needs scouting before you start. And just below here is another drop with a hole all the way across the river that's hard to punch through at high flows. It, too, should have been scouted already. About a quarter mile later is a bigger drop that can be seen from 6200 South just west of the Heather Restaurant. An eddy on the right, just above the drop, is good for landing and portaging.

Below the bridge at 6200 South, right after a sharp left, is a giant cottonwood tree blocking more than half the river. From here down to just above Cottonwood Mall, the river is channeled between cement and gabion walls. This doesn't allow for many eddies, but there are a few because it turns so much. Unfortunately, the turns also make it hard to see far ahead.

When you get to the next bridge (where the road behind the mall crosses), you need to get out. Below here the river is walled in so you can't stop. Before you're committed, walk down to the mall and make sure you can fit under the bridges. Be sure to look partway across the mall parking lot at the diversion dam that is right below a bridge. It can be run at some levels but not others. In high water you won't fit under Highland Drive, and a gate is across the river at the bridge immediately below Highland Drive. The river slows after here as you enter a park. This turns into a lake if the river is too high. Walk around the spillway.

There's a low footbridge and a small drop before 4500 South. Don't go under the bridge at 4500 South without checking it out first. A couple of pipes hidden under there are lower than the bridge.

The river is much slower below here and more suitable for canoeing. You probably won't fit under State Street, but the river is free of obstructions after that and you'll come to the Jordan River a little above 3900 South.

Black's Fork

Map: See p. xxiv.
Difficulty: Class 1 to 3. Fast, small, trees.
Length: East Fork, 6 miles; West Fork, 3.5 miles described.
Time of Year: June.
Average Gradient: East Fork, 73 ft./mi.; West Fork (lower), 83 ft./mi.
Flow Levels: Gage is a mile below confluence of the two forks. Average high is about 1,500 cfs, with a record of 2,480 cfs on 19 June 1983.

Topo Maps: Red Knob, Elizabeth Mountain, Mount Lovenia, Lyman Lake.

Access: Dirt roads from U-150 or from the Fort Bridger-Mountain View area of Wyoming.

First Run: Les Jones, accompanied on some sections by Cal Giddings, Chuck Richards, Klaus Axmor. East Fork—24 May and 23 June 1974; West Fork—24 May, 14 and 23 June, and 13 July 1974.

Black's Fork drains some of the most scenic areas of the north slope of the Uinta Mountains. As on all Uinta rivers, watch out for logjams. In high flows it's probably best to scout everything before running.

EAST FORK OF BLACK'S FORK

A good dirt road takes you to a trailhead just below a ranger (guard) station. A locked gate closes the road beyond here.

The first half mile is Class 2 and then eases to Class 1 and really winds for about 1.5 miles. It then steepens as it straightens, with Class 2 rapids the rest of the way. Watch out for several logjams. On the left about halfway through the run you can see two old, collapsed log cabins.

About a half mile above the confluence with the West Fork, the river splits into many channels until about a half mile after the two rivers come together. Another quarter mile beyond this is a bridge going to the Hewinta Guard Station, a good place to take out.

WEST FORK OF BLACK'S FORK

Because I didn't have the right kind of vehicle for the road conditions, I've not been able to get to the upper parts of the West Fork. Pictures I've seen of it and descriptions I've heard indicate there are a couple of Class 2 to 3 sections alternating with some easy, picturesque meadows and a few deadfall areas that are hard to get through. If you want to run the upper stretches of the river, you will need a high-clearance vehicle.

The lower 3.5 miles are more accessible. Shortly after taking the turnoff going up the West Fork, the dirt road splits. The straight (right) one is the main road. The left one goes a short ways to a bridge and private property. This bridge is a good access point. Above the bridge for about a mile is smooth water through a meadow and then an easy rapid right above the bridge. The river is then smooth as it goes under the bridge and around the first bend where it picks up to Class 2. At a small picnic area about three-quarters mile down, the river splits up a great deal for about a half-mile, and there are several logjams. The channels get so small in spots that a kayak touches both sides. The last mile to the bridge near the confluence is good Class 2 boating.

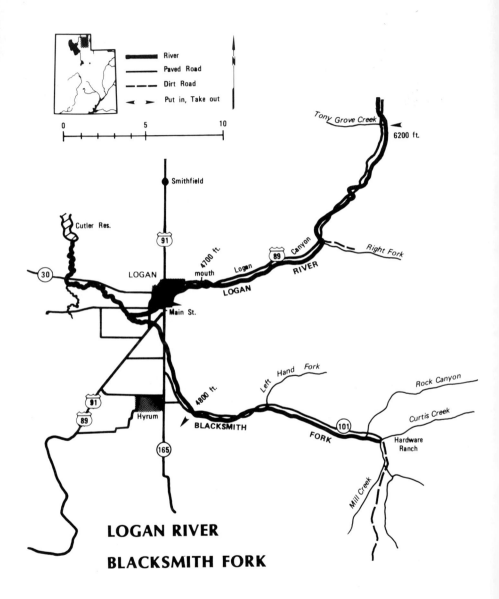

River
Paved Road
Dirt Road
Put in, Take out

0   5   10

N

Tony Grove Creek

6200 ft.

Smithfield

Cutler Res.

91

30

LOGAN

4700 ft.
mouth

Logan

89

Canyon

Right Fork

RIVER

LOGAN

Main St.

Left Hand Fork

Rock Canyon

Curtis Creek

91

89

4800 ft.

Hyrum

BLACKSMITH

101

FORK

Hardware
Ranch

165

Mill Creek

LOGAN RIVER
BLACKSMITH FORK

Blacksmith Fork

Difficulty: Class 1 to 3.
Length: 9 miles from Hardware Ranch to reservoir; 0.5 mile to Hyrum
City Power Plant; 3.75 miles to reservoir; 3 miles to mouth.
Time of Year: Last half of May.
Average Gradient: Upper, 41 ft./mi.; lower, 70 ft./mi.
Flow Levels: Normal high is 500 cfs with a record, 1,620 cfs on 15
May 1917.
Topo Maps: Hardware Ranch, Logan Peak, Porcupine Reservoir, Para-
dise, Logan.
Access: U-101.
First Run: ?

This is a seldom-run, tiny river. It's probably not worth driving a long
way just to run it, but it is worth stopping at on your way to the Logan
River or if you want to spend some time in a nice canyon to do some
camping or fishing.

 The best boating is from a dam and small lake about 4 miles up the
canyon down to its mouth. This is mainly Class 2 with a little Class 3.
Above the dam, the river is slower. A few rapids, a power plant, and a
second dam are encountered. Some beautiful, slow, meandering sections make this part of the river nice for a relaxing float and some good
fishing.

BRUNEAU & JARBIDGE RIVERS

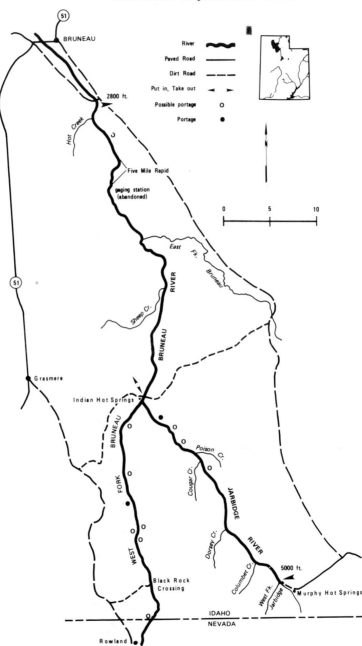

River	
Paved Road	
Dirt Road	
Put in, Take out	
Possible portage	O
Portage	●

51

BRUNEAU

2800 ft.

Hot Creek

Five Mile Rapid

gaging station
(abandoned)

51

East Fk. Bruneau

RIVER

Sheep Cr.

BRUNEAU

Grasmere

Indian Hot Springs

BRUNEAU

O O O

Poison Cr.

FORK

Cougar Cr.

O O

Dorsey Cr.

JARBIDGE

WEST

O O O

RIVER

5000 ft.

Black Rock
Crossing

Columbet Cr.

West Fk. Jarbidge

Murphy Hot Springs

IDAHO
NEVADA

Rowland

0   5   10

Bruneau and Jarbidge Rivers

Difficulty: Class 2 to 4 (one Class 6 rapid). Far from help, a few boulder drops.
Length: Murphy Hot Springs to Indian Hot Springs, about 30 miles; Indian Hot Springs to take-out, about 40 miles.
Time of Year: Late April to June.
Average Gradient: Jarbidge, 35–40 ft./mi.; Bruneau, 30 ft./mi. Both rivers have some sections that are much flatter and some that are much steeper.
Flow Levels: Normal high is around 2,000 cfs with a record of 6,500 cfs on 1 March 1910 at the gage 1 mile downstream from Hot Creek, 9 miles southeast of Bruneau.
Topo Maps: Poison Butte, The Arch, Inside Lake, Indian Hot Springs, Cave Draw, Stiff Tree Draw, Winter Camp, Austin Butte, Crowbar Gulch, Hot Spring, Sugar Valley (also larger series: Winter Camp, Indian Cave, Bruneau).
Access: From Murphy Hot Springs or dirt roads off ID-51.
First Run: ?

These two rivers are as close to the Salt Lake City area as many of the southern Utah runs. They are often run together as part of a three- to five-day trip.

The Bruneau and Jarbidge run through a beautiful wilderness. Take care of it. There isn't anyone to check on you, but river runners are asked to obtain permits from the BLM. Contact: Bureau of Land Management, Boise District Office, 3948 Development Ave., Boise, Idaho 83705; phone (208) 334-1582. They will send you information, a map, and hydrographs.

The usual put-in is about 2 miles below Murphy Hot Springs at the bridge where the west and south forks of the Jarbidge River come together. In high water you can put in before the bridge. Good camping is close by.

Except for those mentioned, most of the rapids on the Jarbidge are Class 1 to 3−. It takes about seven hours boating time to reach the Bruneau. The scenery, especially in the upper section, is very beautiful with sheer basalt walls rising abruptly out of the river.

The BLM lists three possible portages and one definite portage. These are all boulder piles and should be scouted. The first two possible portages are Class 4 to 5− (the narrow slots require portaging most rafts); the third is easier—Class 3. The definite portage is a long, Class 6, steeply dropping, boulder-choked rapid. It's obvious if you watch for a large rock slide on the right. As you approach it you will see a huge boulder that looks like it blocks the whole river. Do not go beyond it. There is a portage trail on the left starting beside the boulder. You may want to start your portage well above here. Watch out for poison ivy. A few scenic camping spots are found just below the portage, but not much in the last couple of miles before the Bruneau.

Indian Hot Springs (complete with a man-made bathtub) is on the left about a mile after you join the Bruneau River. A tortuous, four-wheel-drive road comes down to here from the canyon's west rim. This is the put-in road if you just want to run the Bruneau.

It isn't far from the hot spring to the entrance to Bruneau Canyon, where the basalt walls close in quickly. The first rapid cuts right and goes into an undercut cliff and makes an almost 180-degree turn. A mile or so below here are three drops (Class 3) close together. Most of the river is Class 1 and 2. Sheep Creek enters on the left in about 12 miles and adds water. As you approach the East Fork, which is fairly small, the rapids get harder and more frequent. The canyon opens a little and the rock isn't so smooth and sheer.

Five Mile Rapids is a delightful Class 3 to 4. It starts innocently with a couple of easy drops a little below an old abandoned gaging station on the right (a registration box is here). The rapid is almost continuous for 5 miles with a fair amount of maneuvering required, especially at lower flows.

After Five Mile Rapids ends, the rapids continue but have longer breaks between them. This continues until you reach the last rapid that the BLM lists as a possible portage. You'll know you're there when the river splits around an island and you can't tell for sure where to go. A quick scout on the left will help. Again, watch out for poison ivy. The last good camping spot is probably at the end of this rapid because you're soon in cattle country.

There are still several smaller rapids, and, depending on where you take out, two diversion dams. The first is often run, the second isn't. The bridge after the second dam is a good take-out.

The author works his way through the narrow section of Clear Creek. Neil
Kahn.

16

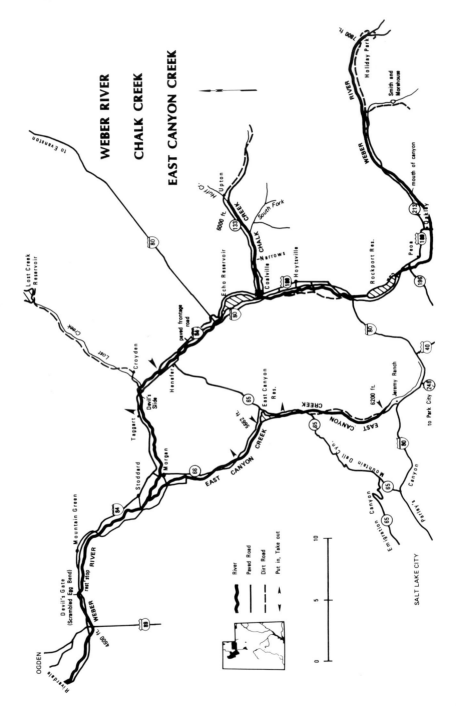

WEBER RIVER

CHALK CREEK

EAST CANYON CREEK

Chalk Creek

Difficulty: Class 1 to 2+.
Length: About 15 miles, with 1 mile of whitewater. Road mostly follows it, so almost any length can be done.
Time of Year: May through mid-June.
Average Gradient: 40 ft./mi.
Flow Levels: Normal high is about 500 cfs with a record of 1,570 cfs on 1 June 1983.
Topo Maps: Coalville, Turner Hollow, Upton.
Access: U-133.
First Run: ? Neil Kahn and Gary Nichols ran some of it, including The Narrows, on 29 May 1985.

Chalk Creek becomes large enough to run where it comes together with the South Fork. There is Class 2 whitewater below there, and then it winds through farmland with occasional riffles, fences, bridges, and diversions. I haven't run all this, but it appears to make for good canoeing. I saw a few trees that had fallen in.

About 2.5 miles above Coalville is a section called the Narrows. This is one of the few spots where the river cannot be seen from the road. The river cuts through a narrow gorge for about a half mile with the road going above and around it.

This little gorge is scenic with fairly swift, Class 2 water. Its brushy banks would make stopping difficult during high water. A bridge just below the Narrows makes a good take-out.

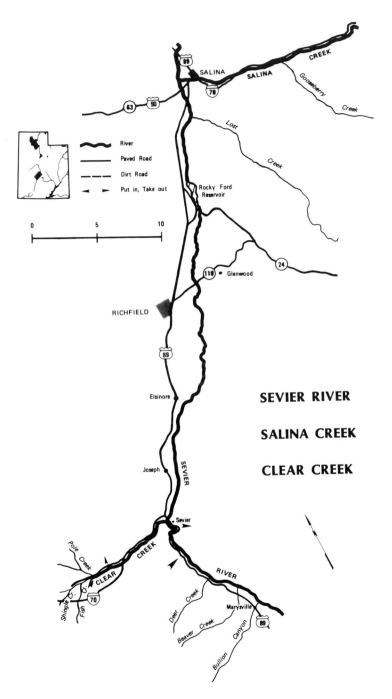

SEVIER RIVER

SALINA CREEK

CLEAR CREEK

Clear Creek

Difficulty: Class 1 to 3. Narrow and rocky in spots with fallen trees in several places. Probably too small for a raft.
Length: Best section about 2 miles. Road follows so longer or shorter lengths possible.
Time of Year: May through June.
Average Gradient: 50 ft./mi.
Flow Levels: Normal peak is around 300 cfs with a record of 769 cfs on 29 April 1973.
Topo Maps: Sevier.
Access: The old highway (Temporary I-70) that connected I-15 and US-89 went right along Clear Creek. Now the interstate bypasses the narrow canyon section so you exit the freeway at the ranch exit by its mouth and take the old highway.
First Run: Neil Kahn and Gary Nichols, 8 May 1985.

The Clear Creek area is interesting both for the narrow scenic canyon and for the ancient Indian ruins and petroglyphs. The river is small but swift. It's possible to put in or take out almost anywhere along its course; however, the creek is too small to run above the confluence with Fish Creek. From the confluence down is about a mile of fast but fairly smooth water with overhanging trees and tight turns. The best rapids are where the creek and road are pinched between cliffs for about a mile. Watch out for trees across the stream, and when the canyon widens expect logjams until reaching the freeway.

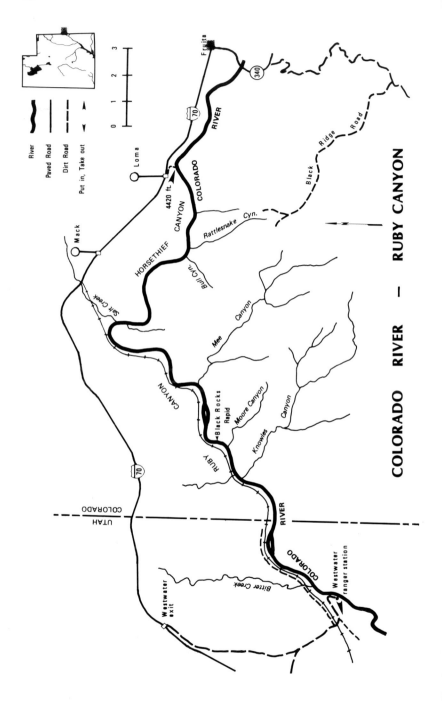

COLORADO RIVER — RUBY CANYON

Colorado River

HORSETHIEF AND RUBY CANYONS

Difficulty: Class 1 to 2, depending on the flow, but mainly flat.
Length: 27 miles.
Time of Year: Year-round, with June having the highest flows.
Average Gradient: 5 ft./mi.
Flow Levels: The average peak for this section is about 25,000 cfs, with a recorded high of 76,800 cfs on 19 June 1917. On 27 May 1984, it reached 69,800 cfs. The all-time record, determined from high-water marks, was 125,000 cfs on 4 July 1884.
Topo Maps: Mack, Ruby Canyon, Bitter Creek Well, Westwater 4SE.
Access: To get to the put-in, take the Loma exit from I-70, turn south, and immediately turn left on a dirt road. Follow it east and down to the river about a half mile to a launch area. To get to the take-out, turn off I-70 at the Westwater exit (or ranch exit to west) and follow the dirt road to the ranger station.
First Run: Frank Kendrick and 4 others, April 1889.

Horsethief Canyon begins about a mile downriver from the put-in. The first 6 miles in the canyon are beautiful. Sandstone cliffs (Entrada, Kayenta, and Wingate) rise up on both sides and several interesting side canyons come in. There are several small rapids through here. The canyon widens out into more open desert country, and Salt Creek comes in at about mile 10, marking the end of Horsethief Canyon. The railroad enters here and follows the river to Westwater.

Ruby Canyon soon starts, and once again the sandstone cliffs appear. At about mile 14, just before Mee Canyon, some interesting balanced rocks and hollowed-out cliffs appear on the left. At about mile 17, you come to Black Rocks Rapid. There really isn't much whitewater here except during spring runoff, but there are a few rocks to dodge and the river funnels through some narrow channels. Inexperienced boaters may want to scout the top part of this. There is a good campsite on the left here where Moore Canyon comes out.

Between miles 19 and 20, you pass the mouth of Knowles Canyon. I've seen a few bald eagles here. The last 4 or 5 miles of the run become more open on the left with several ranches.

Much of the land along the river is privately owned. Contact the BLM District Office, 764 Horizon Dr., Grand Junction, Colorado 81505; phone (303) 243-6552 for information and a map showing private property.

Be sure you get out at the Westwater Ranger Station unless you have a permit and are prepared for Class 3 to 4 whitewater.

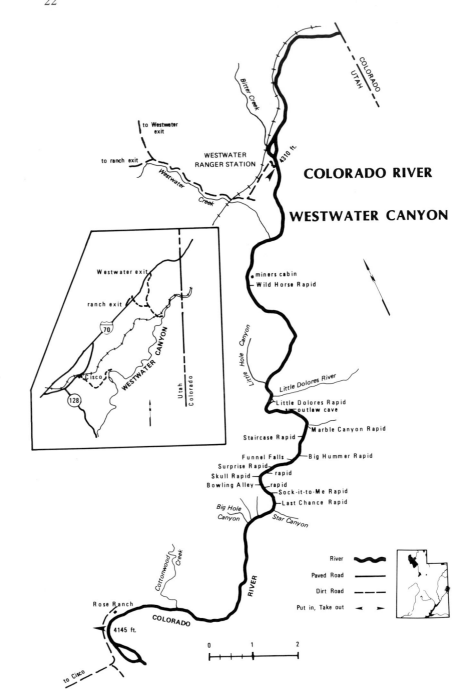

COLORADO
UTAH

to Westwater
exit

to ranch exit

WESTWATER
RANGER STATION

Westwater Creek

Bitter Creek

4310 ft.

COLORADO RIVER

WESTWATER CANYON

Westwater exit

ranch exit

70

Cisco

128

WESTWATER CANYON

Utah
Colorado

• miners cabin
Wild Horse Rapid

Little Hole Canyon

Little Dolores River

Little Dolores Rapid
outlaw cave

Marble Canyon Rapid

Staircase Rapid

Funnel Falls — Big Hummer Rapid
Surprise Rapid
Skull Rapid — rapid
Bowling Alley — rapid
Sock-it-to-Me Rapid
Last Chance Rapid

Big Hole
Canyon

Star Canyon

Cottonwood Creek

RIVER

Rose Ranch

COLORADO

4145 ft.

to Cisco

River	～～～	
Paved Road	——	
Dirt Road	— — —	
Put in, Take out	◄ ►	

0   1   2

WESTWATER CANYON

Difficulty: Class 1 to 4. Short steep drops, sheer walls, holes.
Length: 17 miles.
Time of Year: Year-round, with highest flows usually in June. A permit is required from 1 May through 30 September.
Average Gradient: 9 ft./mi. (21 ft./mi. in the 2.5 miles from Marble Canyon to Star Canyon).
Flow Levels: See Horsethief and Ruby Canyons.
Topo Maps: Westwater 4SE and 4SW, Coates Creek.
Access: Take the Westwater turnoff from I-70 and follow the dirt road to the ranger station. The road can be slick after a good rain. You can also take the ranch exit west of the Westwater exit. A dirt road from the frontage road joins the Westwater road. The take-out is by Cisco near Rose Ranch. Depending on which direction you're coming from, take one of the two Cisco exits off I-70 and follow several miles to Cisco. (Cisco has few inhabitants, with no gas or food available.) At Cisco, take the dirt road going southeast behind the town. In a couple of miles the road splits; take the left fork to the river.
First Run: Ellsworth Kolb and Bert Loper, September 1916.

This is a very popular run for kayaks and rafts. The off-season in low-water years may be difficult for larger rafts. The run can be done easily in a day, but groups often take two. Camping space is limited, though, and the popular places (mainly by the Little Dolores Creek) can be crowded. Several commercial companies run trips through here. For private permit information, contact the Bureau of Land Management, Grand Resource Area, P.O. Box M, Moab, Utah 84532; phone (801) 259-8193.

The first 3 miles of this run are flat through ranch land. The first rapid comes when you reach the massive sandstone cliffs on the right. There is an old dugout cabin on the left a little below the rapid and the remains of a couple of cabins about a half mile farther. The next 4 miles have numerous Class 1 and 2 rapids. Then when the Little Dolores comes in, there are a couple of larger rapids. A short hike up the Little Dolores takes you to a beautiful waterfall and pool. An outlaw cave is on the left about a quarter mile below here.

The real fun starts about a mile below Little Dolores at Marble Canyon. The river narrows with high cliffs on both sides, and in the next 2.5 miles you encounter about ten exciting rapids (Class 3 to 4).

Marble Canyon Rapid is the longest rapid. It is followed by Staircase, which is shorter but has some nice surfing on large standing waves. After a short break with a couple of small drops, Big Hummer appears on a right turn where a large rock blocks the left center in lower water.

Then a short flat water section leads to a rock sticking up on the left and a horizon line marking Funnel Falls. At the bottom of this big drop, waves pound you from both sides and the current carries you toward the cliff on the right. Two short drops—Surprise and an unnamed one—keep the excitement up between Funnel and Skull.

Most people (at least the first time) pull over on the left just above Skull in order to scout from the rocks. At high water this may not be possible in a raft. Below about 3,000 cfs, a gigantic boulder blocks most of the channel, but at higher levels a huge hole is formed. Run it safely on the left, or pay up your life insurance and go for the center of the hole. Just below here the river slams into the cliff and goes left; but on the right a large, circular alcove called the Room of Doom has been cut into the wall. At levels above 6,000 cfs, an extremely strong eddy forms here that has trapped many rafts for hours. To escape, they have sometimes had to persuade a kayaker to ferry a rope across the river so that they could be pulled over the eddyline by people on the other side. I've even seen groups deflate their rafts and haul all their equipment up the cliff and lower it down the other side into the river to escape.

Below Skull is Bowling Alley, where the famous Endo Hole is created at flows up to about 4,500 cfs. Next comes a small unnamed rapid and then Sock-It-To-Me, where a steep drop converges into a crashing wave that does literally what the name suggests. Endos and cartwheels of the deep and instantaneous kind can be done here.

The last major rapid, Last Chance, has a large boulder blocking the center of the river except at flows above about 7,500 cfs, when a huge wave is formed. Two small rapids follow. The first has an excellent endo spot where a ledge comes out from the right. Six miles of flat but scenic water bring you to the take-out below Rose Ranch.

Books: *Canyonlands River Guide* (Westwater Books), by Bill and Buzz Belknap.

The Endo Hole in Westwater Canyon on the Colorado River, enjoyed here by the author, is a favorite play spot for kayakers at flows below 5,000 cfs. Kirk Nichols.

Lane Johnson takes the plunge at the main falls in Black Canyon of the Bear River. Gary Nichols.

The author threads his way through the second possible portage on the Jarbidge River. Lane Johnson.

Canoeists enjoy the quiet beauty found in Ruby Canyon of the Colorado River.
Gary Nichols.

*The deep sandstone canyon carved by the Colorado River above Moab is an
ideal place for canoeing.* Kirk Nichols.

Straight Canyon (Cottonwood Creek) is one of the outstanding advanced kayak runs in Utah. Lane Johnson heads for a slot between rocks on an exploratory run at high water. Gary Nichols.

The huge waves of Big Drop 3 in Cataract Canyon pound a 30-foot J Rig. Kirk Nichols.

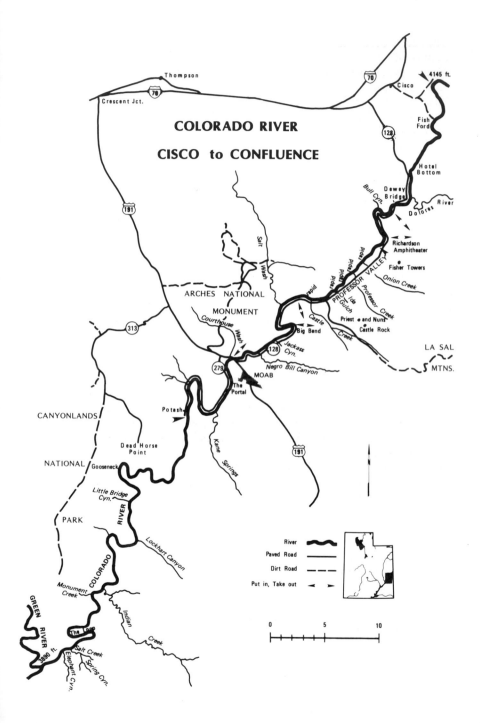

COLORADO RIVER

CISCO to CONFLUENCE

Thompson

Crescent Jct.

Cisco

4145 ft.

Fish Ford

Hotel Bottom

Dewey Bridge

River

Bull Cyn.

Dolores

Richardson Amphitheater

Fisher Towers

Onion Creek

PROFESSOR VALLEY

Professor Creek

Salt Wash

rapid

Ida Gulch

ARCHES NATIONAL

MONUMENT

Courthouse

Castle

Priest and Nuns

Castle Rock

Big Bend

Castle Creek

LA SAL

MTNS.

Wash

Jackass Cyn.

MOAB

Negro Bill Canyon

The Portal

Potash

CANYONLANDS

Dead Horse Point

Kane Springs

NATIONAL

Gooseneck

Little Bridge Cyn.

PARK

COLORADO RIVER

Lockhart Canyon

Monument Creek

Indian Creek

GREEN RIVER

3890 ft.

The Loop

Salt Creek

Elephant Cyn.

Spring Cyn.

River

Paved Road

Dirt Road

Put in, Take out

0   5   10

CISCO TO MOAB

Difficulty: Class 1 to 3.
Length: 47 miles.
Time of Year: Year-round.
Average Gradient: 3.5 ft./mi.
Flow Levels: See Horsethief and Ruby Canyons.
Topo Maps: Coates Creek, Cisco, Castle Valley, Moab.
Access: U-128 follows the river.
First Run: Frank Kendrick and 4 others, April 1889.

After exiting from Westwater Canyon, the Colorado River flows smoothly for 25 miles until Onion Creek, where it is once again broken by rapids as far as Jackass Creek, after which it flows smoothly past Moab and on to Cataract Canyon. This trip can be made as a continuation of a Westwater trip, or separately by putting in at the usual Westwater take-out or almost anywhere from the Dewey Bridge to Moab.

At first, the river is broken into channels by several islands, then it flows together past Fish Ford and on to the islands at Hotel Bottom, after which the Dewey Road (U-128) comes in from the northwest. This road follows the river the rest of the way to Moab and is now paved except at two creek bottoms that often wash out in flash floods. More permanent culverts are being installed so the road may soon be all paved.

The Dolores River joins the Colorado from the east, and about a half mile below this is a small arch high on the left wall. This was the Dewey area, a small ranching community in the late 1800s. The BLM has a trolley across the river here with a gaging station on the east side. The Dewey Bridge, an interesting old single-lane suspension bridge, crosses the river another half mile downstream. A few ancient Indian petroglyphs highlight the area.

The canyon walls rise and narrow, forming a short canyon of Wingate Sandstone for 6 miles below Dewey. About halfway through and on the right is Bull Canyon, a beautiful side hike to a usually dry waterfall.

The Fisher Towers and the La Sal Mountains come into view as the canyon widens into the Richardson Amphitheatre. As the river enters Professor Valley, a prominent butte called The Priest and Nuns comes into view along with Castle Rock.

Several access points to the river are available along here. One is from the road just opposite the Fisher Tower Road, and another is about a mile farther upstream. This upper one is used heavily by commercial raft companies for put-ins for the ''daily'' section. If you have a raft this is the easiest put-in.

During the high spring runoff, the five rapids below can develop large waves and strong undertows. Onion Creek and Professor Creek rapids are simple enough. A mile below these is a new rapid that was formed by a flash flood during a thunderstorm in the summer of 1976. This rapid has several names, but Cloudburst seems most appropriate. This is the most difficult rapid at most levels. It's against a cliff on the left and should be scouted on the right by those in open craft. There are undertows at the bottom left with a large whirlpool forming at very high flows. The right side is rocky.

A dirt road comes down to the river at Ida Gulch, making this a good access point. The rapid here is rocky at low flows; at higher flows the river runs forcefully into the right wall.

Another possible access point is a short dirt road that leaves U-128 across from the Castle Valley Road. It was damaged by high water in 1984 and may not be in good shape. Below this turnoff the river is straight for nearly a mile until the White Ranch where it makes a sharp right and then a sharp left where White's or Castle Creek Rapid starts. In medium high water this has some huge waves and a couple of holes.

Below Castle Creek, the river enters another deep canyon and keeps its speed up for several miles, providing excellent intermediate canoeing. A mile below White's Rapid is a BLM landing on the left.

Salt Wash enters from the river's right at Arches National Park boundary. A small rapid is found here in low water. Delicate Arch is an 8-mile hike up the wash. The canyon rim, with its spectacular view of the river, can be reached by hiking south from the end of the road going into the Windows section of Arches.

At Big Bend you will find stone tables and a good access point to the river. The last of several small rapids is just below here at Jackass Creek, and from there to Moab is flat water. Along this section one passes Negro Bill Canyon with its year-round clear stream and excellent hiking. Updraft Arch is high on the left wall about a mile above the Moab Bridge. A concrete landing is on the river's right a few hundred yards above the bridge. U-128 joins US 191 (163) at the southeast end of the bridge.

Books: *Canyonlands River Guide* (Westwater Books), Bill and Buzz Belknap.

MOAB TO LAKE POWELL (CATARACT CANYON)

Difficulty: Class 1 to 4+. Huge waves, big holes in Cataract Canyon.

Length: 112 miles from the Moab Bridge to Hite. Plan on at least 5 to 6 days.

Time of Year: Year-round, but highest flows are in late May and June.

Average Gradient: 1.1 ft./mi. from Moab to Spanish Bottom; 16 ft./mi. from Spanish Bottom to Lake Powell.

Flow Levels: The average peak below the confluence is about 45,000 cfs, with a record of 110,500 cfs on 27 May 1984. Watermarks indicate it was higher than this before records were kept.

Topo Maps: Moab, Hatch Point, Upheaval Dome, Needles, Orange Cliffs, Mouth of Dark Canyon, Brown's Rim, or the large Canyonlands National Park and Vicinity, Utah (1968).

Access: The put-in is at the bridge near Moab where US-191 crosses the Colorado River or at the end of the Potash Road (U-279) which follows the river for 15 miles. The take-out at Hite is on Lake Powell.

First Run: Moab to Confluence—Frank C. Kendrick, late April, early May 1889; below Confluence—John Wesley Powell, J. C. Sumner, William H. Dunn, W. H. Powell, G. Y. Bradley, O. G. Howland, Seneca Howland, W. R. Hawkins, Andrew Hall, July 1869.

A boat ramp just above the US-191 bridge on the north side (described as the take-out for the last section) provides a good put-in. A few hundred yards below the bridge, Courthouse Wash, which drains the southwest corner of Arches National Park, enters the river from the north. Some excellent pictographs and petroglyphs of the Anasazi Indians are on the eastern wall where the wash breaks from the cliffs.

About 2.5 miles below the bridge and after passing through the Moab Valley, the river enters another canyon through The Portal. In the next several miles, petroglyphs, ruins, and arches can be found on both sides of the river. Twelve miles down is the Texas-Gulf potash plant. A road (U-279) goes to here from US-191. The launching area just past the potash plant is the most frequently used put-in for Cataract Canyon.

The river runs smoothly and slowly past Dead Horse Point, towering nearly 2,000 feet above to the north, then continues on around the Goosenecks, widely known from the many published photos taken from Dead Horse Point. Numerous petrified logs can be found on the right bank behind the tamarisk trees before the river turns right at the Goosenecks. As you pass the far side of the Gooseneck, the right bank becomes the boundary for Canyonlands National Park and is marked with a sign. Below here and a mile above Little Bridge Canyon, the river itself enters Canyonlands National Park. This boundary is marked inconspicuously by a sign on the east (left) bank.

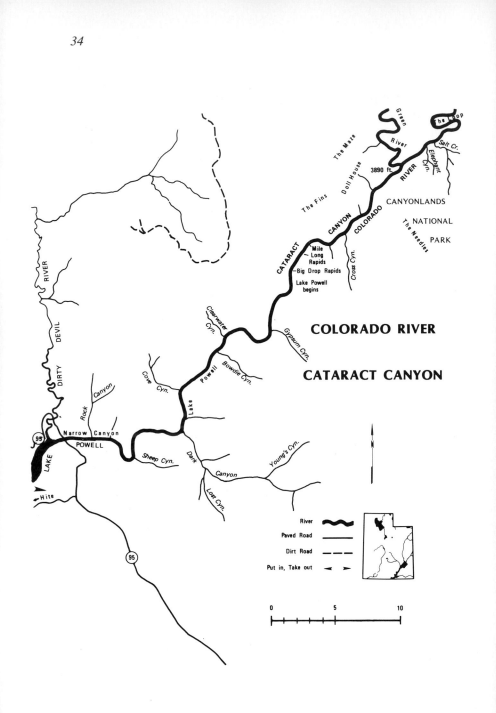

COLORADO RIVER

CATARACT CANYON

Lathrup Canyon enters from the right. Across the river to the south and upstream a short distance are some Indian granaries and pictographs. A four-wheel-drive road comes off the White Rim Trail and down Lathrup Canyon to the river.

On the north wall at the mouth of Indian Creek are several granaries, and 1.5 miles below on the west (right) side of the river is Monument Creek. The right-hand fork leads to Monument Basin and the Totem Pole, a 305-foot stone spire.

At The Loop, the river winds back on itself three times in about four river miles before continuing on. A half-mile hiking trail crosses over the first neck while the river takes 4 miles to go around. If you take the hike watch the larger boulders on the way down; some have faint petroglyphs.

Salt Creek and Elephant Canyon come down from the Needles District of the park and enter the river on the left. Both canyons have granaries at their mouths. Below Elephant Canyon 1.5 miles is The Slide. The right-hand wall has sloughed down, partially blocking the river and creating a riffle. The Green River joins the Colorado another 1.5 miles below The Slide.

A permit from Canyonlands National Park is required for travel on the river below the Confluence. Contact: Superintendent, Canyonlands National Park, Moab, Utah 84532; phone (801) 259-7164.

Cataract Canyon, the "Graveyard of the Colorado," has been the scene of many lost boats and lost lives. There are many inscriptions telling of disaster in places such as Mile-Long Rapid and the Big Drops.

The rapids in Cataract Canyon are different from most on the Colorado. Nearly all are formed by sloughs of hard rock from the narrow canyon walls instead of the usual dams of flash-flood debris from side canyons.

Running Cataract Canyon at high and low water stages is like running two different rivers with different rapids between the same canyon walls. The twenty-five surviving rapids will, in high water, rival the size of the rapids in the Grand Canyon. But in low water, never-ending rocks and tortuous channels characterize the river. The early trips made around the turn of the century were done in the fall, and it was during this low-water time that the blind, left-hand slot in Big Drop 3 acquired the name Satan's Gut.

Lake Powell has been allowed to back up 26 miles into Cataract Canyon, covering over half the rapids, including the once formidable Dark Canyon Rapid. It's hard to find campsites through this section.

Books and maps: *River Runner's Guide to Canyonlands National Park and Vicinity* by Felix Matschler (A Powell Society Publication); *Canyonlands River Guide* by Bill and Buzz Belknap.

GRAND CANYON

River running in the Grand Canyon requires its own book, and as several already cover it I won't go into detail here. This is one of the ultimate runs. Many places have more difficult and dangerous rapids, but few have bigger waves. This, however, is just one aspect that makes the canyon so fantastic. Very few places are left where you can travel more than 200 miles without seeing a dam or passing a town or road. For the most part, the Grand Canyon is still a wilderness area, and most river runners take very good care of it. There are also many years' worth of side canyons to hike and explore.

Permits are required for private parties, and the waiting list is several years long. If you are willing to pay a commercial operator to take you, however, there is no waiting. I am not against commercial operations. Most are very concerned about protecting the rivers and their surrounding areas. Unfortunately, under the present system the distribution of permits between commercial and private boaters is most inequitable.

For information on the Grand Canyon, contact: Superintendent, Grand Canyon National Park, Grand Canyon, Arizona 86023; phone (602) 638-2411.

The following are excellent books and guides on the Grand Canyon. Most guidebooks classify the rapids on a 1-to-10 basis. A 10 roughly equals a 4+ on the scale used in this guide.

Books: George C. Simmons and David L. Gaskill, *River Runner's Guide to the Canyons of the Green and Colorado Rivers, with Emphasis on Geologic Features*, Vol. 3, *Marble Gorge and Grand Canyon* (Powell Society); Buzz Belknap, *Grand Canyon River Guide* (Westwater Books); John Blaustein, Edward Abbey, and Martin Litton, *The Hidden Canyon—A River Journey*. On the Colorado River: *Down the Colorado: Diary of John Wesley Powell*, photographs and epilogue by Eliot Porter; John Wesley Powell, *Exploration of the Colorado River and Its Canyons;* Michael Jenkinson, *Wild Rivers of North America;* W. Kenneth Hamblin and J. Keith Rigby, *Guidebook to the Colorado River*, Parts 1 and 2; Larry Stevens, *The Colorado River in Grand Canyon: A Guide;* Kim Crumbo, *A River Runner's Guide to the History of the Grand Canyon.*

38

SAN RAFAEL RIVER   COTTONWOOD CREEK
FERRON CREEK   PRICE   HUNTINGTON CREEK

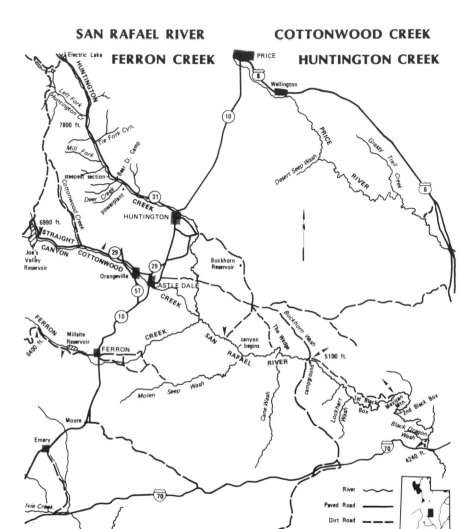

Cottonwood Creek

Difficulty: Class 3 to 4. Large boulders, a few trees, tight turns.
Length: 8 miles.
Time of Year: Usually best in June; dam-controlled.
Average Gradient: 82 ft./mi.
Flow Levels: Normal high is 500 to 600 cfs with a record of 7,220 cfs on 1 August 1964 before the dam was built.
Topo Maps: Joe's Valley Reservoir, Mahogany Point, Red Point.
Access: U-29.
First Run: Gary Nichols and Lane Johnson, 23 June 1984.

This has to be one of the very best advanced kayak runs in Utah. The water comes from the high peaks on the east side of the Wasatch Plateau and is impounded by Joe's Valley Reservoir. It leaves the reservoir clear and cold, a beautiful turquoise color. For 5 miles the river goes through Straight Canyon, pooling above and cascading over and around giant boulders. At high water this is almost all Class 4 with one or two 4+ rapids. It becomes a little easier in lower flows and can almost all be scouted from the road. Put in from the trail leading to the base of the dam or about a mile down where the road drops close to river level. There's a tree across the river at this lower put-in. One of the hardest rapids to find a route through is between the two put-ins.

Actually, the river is not Cottonwood Creek until after Straight Canyon ends. As the canyon widens, Cottonwood Creek enters and the river goes away from the road for about a mile. The river eases some with mostly Class 2 and 3 rapids and a little Class 4. Then it narrows again after swinging back to the road and becomes mostly Class 3 to 4 for about a mile. The rapids pretty much end between mileposts 12 and 13 with one last tough, rocky rapid. From here to Castle Dale is Class 1 and 2 with some diversions.

The only problem with this run is the short boating season. Really high water—above 1,000 cfs—seems rare. Most peaks average 500 cfs or less and may only last a few days to a few weeks depending on reservoir level and snowpack. In high water years it may be runnable for over a month; 300 cfs is about the minimum flow for boating. Cottonwood Creek is a small mountain stream, so watch out for logs.

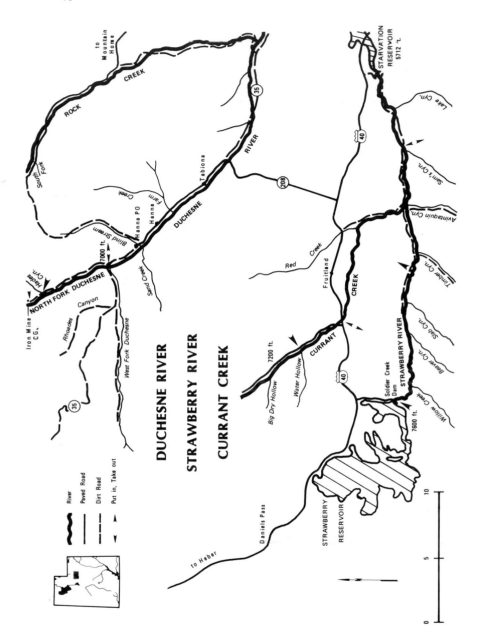

DUCHESNE RIVER

STRAWBERRY RIVER

CURRANT CREEK

River
Paved Road
Dirt Road
Put in, Take out

Currant Creek

Difficulty: Class 1 to 2+.
Length: 25 miles from Dry Hollow to confluence with Strawberry River; 16 miles from US-40 to Strawberry River.
Time of Year: May, June.
Average Gradient: 44 ft./mi.
Flow Levels: Normal high is about 400 cfs with a record of 1,260 cfs on 4 May 1952.
Topo Maps: Raspberry Knoll, Deep Creek, Fruitland, Strawberry Pinnacles.
Access: US-40, Currant Creek Reservoir Road, and Red Creek Road.
First Run: Below US-40—Les Jones, Spring 1974; above US-40— Gary Nichols, Lane Johnson, and Joe Marty, 2 July 1983.

The upper part of Currant Creek below Currant Creek Dam spreads out through meadows and would be difficult to get through. There are a couple of bridges below the meadows that make good put-ins. The river is mostly Class 1 here with a few Class 2 rapids. The harder rapids seem to come when the river is closest to the road. Expect to find several trees blocking the river.

Below US-40, the river parallels the highway for a short way and is ugly with debris and old cars. It gets prettier as you move away from the highway, meandering through farm and ranch land.

After several miles you come to a narrower canyon that has some fairly technical Class 2 rapids at the start. It soon opens up into an area with summer homes. Then you enter a second narrow canyon that continues to where the Red Creek road comes in. The best rapids are again toward the beginning, the current slowing just before Red Creek enters. This creek is hardly noticeable most of the time, but after it joins, the river is no longer called Currant Creek but is now Red Creek. After about a mile of flat water, the gradient steepens with several Class 2+ to 3− drops near some large pipes. The river stays fast until the confluence with the Strawberry River.

Watch out for logs. A couple were across the river in the last few miles when I ran it. If the river is above 2.5 on the gage at US-40, the last few miles will have some pretty good waves. If the gage is below 2.0, this last section will be shallow.

Dirty Devil River

Difficulty: Class 1 to 2. Far from help.
Length: 51 miles to Poison Spring Road; 84 miles to Hite Marina.
Time of Year: Usually early June.
Average Gradient: 8.5 ft./mi.
Flow Levels: Normal high is 500 to 600 cfs with a record of 35,000 cfs on 4 November 1957. The gage is by the Poison Spring Wash Road on the right bank.
Topo Maps: Hanksville, Robber's Roost Canyon, Fiddler Butte, Brown's Rim.
Access: U-95, dirt road to Poison Spring Draw, and Lake Powell.
First Run: ?

The Dirty Devil River begins where the Fremont River and Muddy Creek come together near Hanksville. The road crosses the river here. At first the scenery is not very impressive and neither is the river. Unless you're lucky and get some very high water, you may have to walk through shallows fairly often in the first 10 miles—and you'll probably think of worse names than "Dirty Devil" to call the river.

It's about 15 miles to Robber's Roost Canyon. By this time you are well into the Navajo Sandstone where the scenery is spectacular and the river quits spreading out, though the riverbed still remains wide. This canyon occasionally carries as much water as the Grand Canyon. Flash floods have turned this calm, shallow stream into a raging torrent of over 20,000 cfs a number of times, and thus the wide riverbed. But mostly, you're lucky to have 500 cfs.

Most of the river is flat water with fairly frequent small sand waves and occasional rocky riffles at the mouths of side canyons. The water speeds up and has more rapids after Happy Canyon, 28 miles past Robber's Roost. Nice campsites abound, but clear running water is almost nonexistent. It's best to carry all your drinking water with you. As there are many beautiful side canyons, allow time for hiking.

The road from Poison Spring Canyon comes to the river about a mile above the actual mouth to Poison Spring Canyon. This is about 8 miles below Happy Canyon. The road requires four-wheel-drive or at least a very low gear to get up the steep hills.

Lake Powell's currentless water is another 13 miles beyond here if the lake is full. About the same time you run out of current, it seems a strong upstream wind hits you, making forward progress even harder. One nice thing about getting to the lake is that the water becomes clear and you can finally get clean when you wash. It's possible to take out on a rough road soon after reaching the lake, or you can continue for about

20 miles to Hite Marina. Partway through this last section is a giant, permanent-looking logjam, probably 200 yards long. A hard-hulled boat can push the debris aside; a raft or inflatable kayak might have trouble getting through.

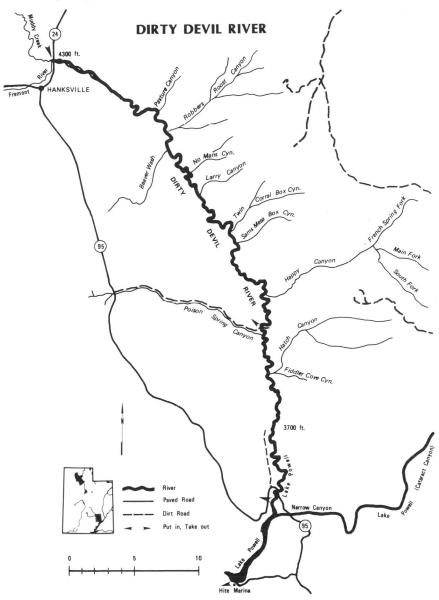

DIRTY DEVIL RIVER

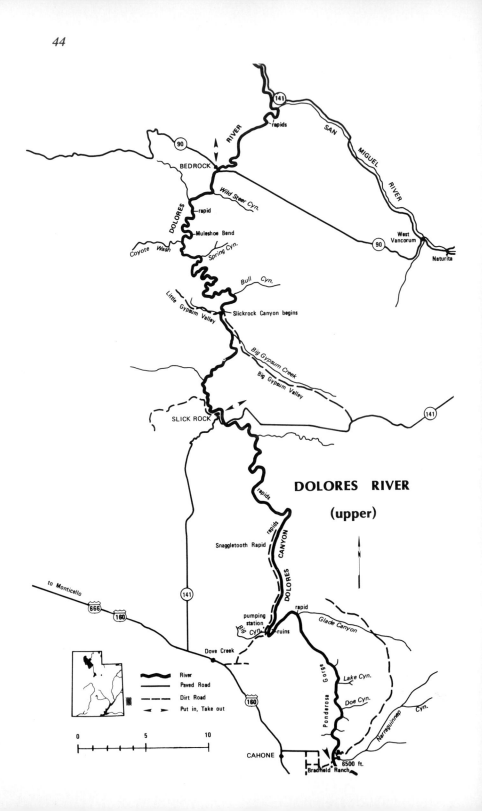

DOLORES RIVER

(upper)

Dolores River

Difficulty: Class 2 to 4.
Length: Cahone to Slickrock, 50 miles; Slickrock to Bedrock, 45 miles; Gateway to Colorado River, 32 miles.
Time of Year: April through June; dam-controlled.
Average Gradient: Cahone to Slickrock, 20 ft./mi. (60 ft./mi. at Snaggletooth); Slickrock to Bedrock, 10 ft./mi.; Gateway to Colorado River, 13 ft./mi. (60 ft./mi. at Stateline Rapid and 40 ft./mi. for the next 2 miles).
Flow Levels: The average peak is about 8,000 cfs in late April or early May, with a record high of 17,400 cfs on 21 April 1958. The gage is 9 miles upstream from the mouth of the river.
Topo Maps: Doe Canyon, The Glade, Secret Canyon, Joe Davis Hill, Slickrock, Anderson Mesa, Paradox, Gateway, Coates Creek, Polar Mesa, Cisco.
Access: Put in at Gateway, Colorado, where C-141 crosses the river, and take out at the Dewey Bridge northeast of Moab. The shuttle is long and takes 3 to 4 hours to drive. It can be done several ways. The fastest paved route is to take C-141 northeast to Grand Junction and then follow I-70 to Cisco, where you take U-128 south to the Dewey Bridge. The other way is more scenic, taking you around the La Sal Mountains. Go south on C-141 and then on C-90 through Bedrock to La Sal on U-46, then take US-163 to Moab and U-128 to the Dewey Bridge. There is also a more direct route on a dirt road that goes through the La Sal Mountains to Castle Valley (see map).
First Run: Otis "Doc" and Margaret Marston, Preston and Becky Walker, May 1948.

CAHONE TO BEDROCK

The Dolores offers a lot of variety. How good the river running will be depends on how much water is released from the recently completed dam. The most popular stretch is from Cahone to Slickrock. The first few miles are flat but have good current. When you come to a grove of ponderosa pine on the right, the rapids start getting better. Beautiful campsites are plentiful from here until the ponderosa end about a mile above the pumping station. At Glade Canyon you come to several good rapids, the river making a major swing left here. Just before it swings back to the right (about a half mile above the pumping station) are some Indian ruins on the right about a hundred feet up where a ledge runs along the cliff.

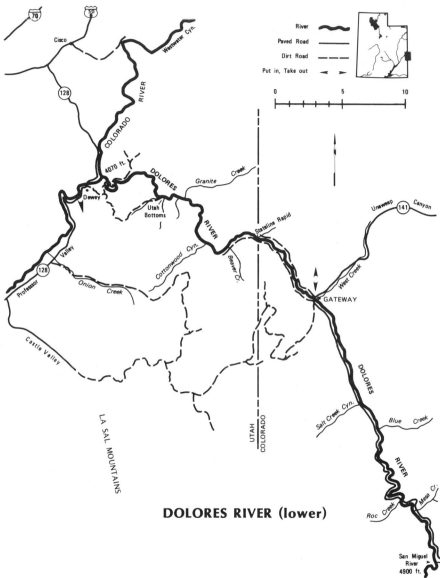

DOLORES RIVER (lower)

Snaggletooth Rapid (Class 3+ to 4+ depending on water level) is about 7 miles below the pumping station. To recognize Snaggletooth in time to stop, watch downriver until you see a pointed, conical mountain. You then have about 200 yards to land on the left and scout. Especially in high water, the rapids below Snaggletooth are fun and almost continuous for several miles. Dolores Canyon reaches its deepest point near here. The next 20 miles or so have rapids scattered throughout, the canyon then opening out into a desert valley at Slickrock.

Below Slickrock the desert scenery is spectacular. There are fewer rapids and most of them are fairly easy. Experienced canoeists often run this stretch. Pictographs and petroglyphs can be found through here. In much of Slickrock Canyon you'll be more than 1,000 feet below the rim, often with sheer sandstone walls rising straight out of the river. Several side canyons offer excellent hiking. The usual take-out is at Bedrock.

GATEWAY TO COLORADO RIVER

This section is mostly in Utah and isn't run as often as the Cahone to Bedrock sections. Much of it is wilderness and some is isolated ranching country.

The first few miles are flat and fairly slow until you come to a short, almost vertical drop. A long, Class 2 rapid starts after this with several more small rapids in the next few miles. Just before the canyon narrows, you come to Stateline Rapid. You'll hear it and see a big boulder on the right and another big boulder with flat sides on the left next to a dirt road. This rapid should be scouted. It's pretty wild (Class 4) at high water, with several big holes and large waves. Since it goes around a couple of bends before it ends, you can't see most of it from the top.

Several more good rapids are encountered in the next few miles; most would be difficult in an open canoe at high water. The rest of the way, the rapids are smaller and there's more time to enjoy the canyon view. The dirt road is lost finally as the canyon narrows. A few campsites are found along here as are many more as the canyon opens up. At about mile 20 (Utah Bottoms), a large canyon comes in from the left where several buildings and a gage are located. A couple of miles below this is the last good rapid (Class 2), the final few miles before the Colorado River proving very slow.

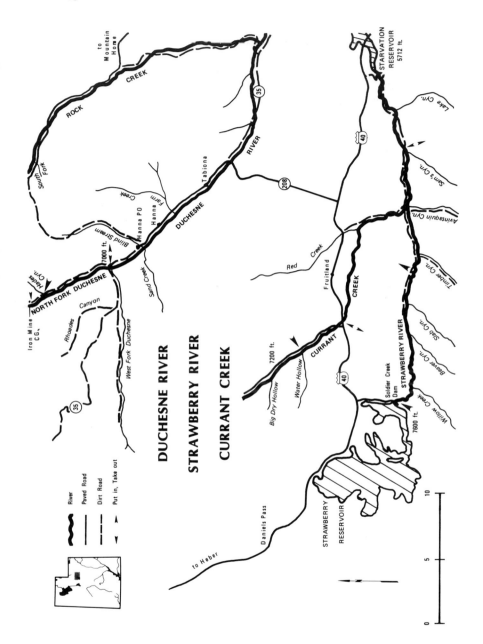

DUCHESNE RIVER

STRAWBERRY RIVER

CURRANT CREEK

River
Paved Road
Dirt Road
Put in, Take out

Duchesne River

Difficulty: Class 1 to 3. Narrow, trees, small dams, mostly too small for rafts.

Length: North Fork, 6.5 miles from Hades Campground to West Fork; main Duchesne, 6.5 miles to Hanna and another 20 miles to Rock Creek.

Time of Year: June

Average Gradient: North Fork, 62 ft./mi.; main Duchesne, 40 ft./mi.

Flow Levels: The normal high for the main Duchesne is about 1,400 cfs with a record of 5,260 cfs on 16 June 1963. (The gage is on the left bank on the upstream side of the bridge on U-35, 7 miles southeast of Tabiona.) The North Fork contributes about two-thirds of the main Duchesne's flow (there's no USGS gage on this section, but see description for other gage).

Topo Maps: Iron Mine Mountain, Granddaddy Lake, Hanna, Blacktail Mountain, Talmage.

Access: U-208, U-35, and dirt road along the North Fork.

First Run: North Fork—Dave Hildebrand and Gary Nichols, 25 June 1984. Main Duchesne—?

NORTH FORK OF THE DUCHESNE

This is the most scenic and exciting section of the Duchesne. It is first accessible from the Mirror Lake Highway (U-150) near Trial Lake on the dirt road going to the east portal of the Duchesne tunnel. Immediately below the small lake at the portal is Cataract Gorge, a steep and narrow section cascading over several falls and dropping 160 feet in the first half mile. This appears to be unrunnable. There is no road access for the next 3 miles, which is mainly Class 2 water.

A dirt road comes up the river from its confluence with the West Fork and ends at Iron Mine Campground. Because of the difficulty of getting around Cataract Gorge (and because of the long shuttle from the east portal of the Duchesne tunnel to the West Fork), this is a better place to put in. The next two miles are mostly flat through meadows until Hades Campground, which is another good put-in.

Most of the river is Class 1 and 2, with one Class 2+ rapid next to the road. Much of it is delightful advanced canoeing. Watch out for logjams and two dams, though. The first dam, about halfway through the run, can be seen from the road and is usually runnable. The second is about a mile farther down (about a half mile below Aspen Campground) and is more obviously a dam, with cement sides. It diverts water into the Rhodes canal, and is easy to walk around.

A gage can be found at the bridge just above the confluence with the West Fork. A good medium level for boating is 3.1 feet on the gage (approximately 500 cfs).

MAIN DUCHESNE

The Duchesne River begins where the north and west forks come together. From here, the river flows through farms and past small towns. The best stretch, Class 1 with a little Class 2, is from the start to about where Rock Creek comes in. This is still in somewhat of a canyon. Below here the canyon opens more and the river becomes mainly slow and meandering, especially after the Strawberry River enters near the town of Duchesne.

It's about 6.5 miles to the town of Hanna from the confluence of the two forks and about 20 more to the confluence with Rock Creek. Watch out for low bridges, logs, fences, and diversions.

East Canyon Creek

Difficulty: Class 1 and 2. Trees, fences, narrow, mostly too small for rafts.
Length: Upper section, 11.5 miles (2 to 3 hours); lower section, 5 miles (1 to 2 hours).
Time of Year: May, and sometimes late April and early June.
Average Gradient: Upper, 45 ft./mi.; lower, 60 ft./mi, with some steeper and more gradual sections.
Flow Levels: 1983 was the first full year records were kept. The high was 531 cfs on 1 June of that year, and the 1984 high flow was 679 cfs on 18 April.
Topo Maps: Big Dutch Hollow, East Canyon Reservoir, Porterville, Morgan.
Access: Upper—dirt road off I-80 between Jeremy Ranch and U-65; lower—U-66.
First Run: Upper—Les Jones, 23 June 1978; lower—Gary Nichols, 18 February 1985.

JEREMY RANCH TO EAST CANYON RESERVOIR

Here is another little stream not far from the Salt Lake City area. It is fairly fast and meandering. The first few miles below Jeremy Ranch are Class 1 water. A couple of pipes must be passed through at the beginning, with a barbed-wire fence across the creek immediately after the second pipe. You'll have to walk around the fence. There are two more fences in the next mile which you can probably squeeze under. About halfway through the run is a fourth fence and near U-65 is a fifth one that is hard to get under.

The second half of this run is narrower with many bushes and branches hanging over both sides. About 1.5 miles before coming to U-65 is a red clay bank on the right. From here down is almost solid Class 2 with some tricky turns and a few rocks to dodge. Just past a farmhouse near where you encounter U-65 are a couple of giant cottonwood trees all the way across the river. U-65 crosses the river in about a mile and is a possible take-out. The river then goes past the condominiums at East Canyon Resort and through a pipe under a dirt road. When the lake is full it backs up almost to here, making this a good take-out.

EAST CANYON RESERVOIR TO BRIDGE

This section is about 5 river miles long, or 4 miles by road. A dirt road takes you near the base of the dam at East Canyon Reservoir. A gate at the entrance is usually locked, but it's not too far to carry a boat.

52

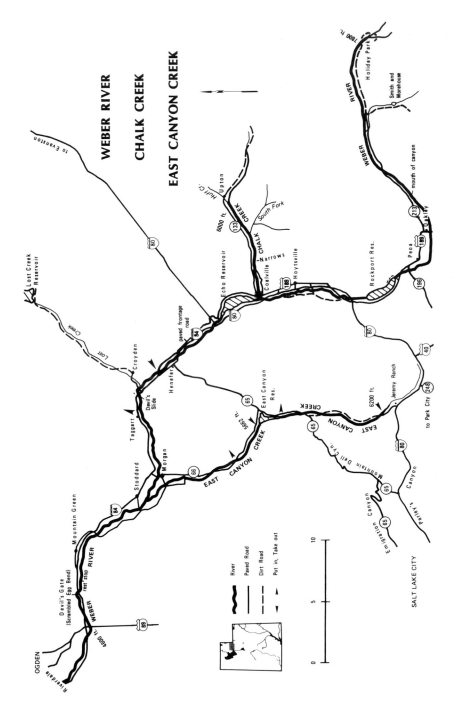

WEBER RIVER

CHALK CREEK

EAST CANYON CREEK

to Evanston

Lost Creek Reservoir

Lost Creek

Croyden

Henefer

paved frontage road

Devil's Slide

Taggert

Stoddard

Morgan

Mountain Green

rest stop

Devil's Gate (Scrambled Egg Bend)

WEBER RIVER

OGDEN

Riverdale

4600 ft.

84

89

66

EAST CANYON CREEK

5652 ft.

65

East Canyon Res.

EAST CANYON CREEK

Mountain Dell Cyn.

Emigration Canyon

65

65

80

Parley's Canyon

SALT LAKE CITY

to Park City

Jeremy Ranch

6200 ft.

248

40

80

196

Peoa

189

213

Oakley

Rockport Res.

Hoytville

189

Coalville

Narrows

Echo Reservoir

80

64

Echo Reservoir

CHALK CREEK

133

6000 ft.

Upton

Huff C.

South Fork

WEBER RIVER

mouth of canyon

Smith and Morehouse

Holiday Park

7800 ft.

River
Paved Road
Dirt Road
Put in, Take out

0   5   10

The canyon is fairly narrow with heavily wooded sections along the river. Many overhanging branches and trees partially block the river—a few of them all the way across.

The gradient is steady, so there are no major drops and very few large rocks. Most of the river is fairly constant Class 1 to 2+ with small waves, the first mile being steepest. After the first right bend is an old diversion, the river hitting the right wall and going left. A cement channel is on the right. The left side was runnable, something you can scout from the put-in road. About a quarter mile farther on is a gage and a low-head dam with a reversal all the way across. You'll probably want to portage this. A dirt road comes down to here.

Probably the only spot that is a distinct rapid is a short section just below a private picnic area. This is Class 2 and a little steeper and rockier than the rest of the river.

Most of the land along the river is private property. Two ranches near the end of the run have posted No Trespassing signs along the river. Several summer homes have been built along this last stretch, as well as two bridges you'll probably have to walk around. There is also a bridge earlier in the run that is high enough to get under at most water levels. Barbed-wire fences are found immediately above and below the take-out bridge.

The canyon opens into farmland below the bridge, with fences, bridges, and trees blocking the river at several spots.

54

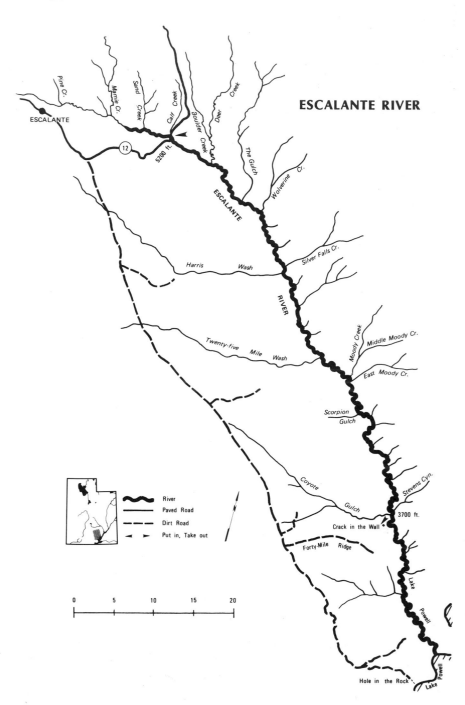

ESCALANTE RIVER

Escalante River

Difficulty: Class 1 and 2. Rocky, far from help, small.
Length: 70 miles from Calf Creek to Coyote Gulch.
Time of Year: Usually about April or May.
Average Gradient: 21 ft./mi.; steepest above The Gulch and below Scorpion Gulch.
Flow Levels: The USGS gage is high up the river near the town of Escalante. So many side streams come in below affecting the flow that this gage isn't very useful. An unmonitored gage at the Calf Creek bridge gives a better idea, but you have to drive there to read it or have someone else go there. The best bet is to call the National Park Service or the Bureau of Land Management in Escalante (see description below). The normal high is only a few hundred cfs.
Topo Maps: Calf Creek, King Bench, Red Breaks, Moody Creek, King Mesa, The Rincon.
Access: U-12, dirt road to Hole in the Rock, and Lake Powell.
First Run: Les Jones, Cal and Steve Giddings, and J. and John Dewell, 14–20 June 1975.

The Escalante River is not quite the pristine wilderness I had expected. Cattle sometimes roam the canyons in the winter, and their smell may linger even though all but dead ones will probably have moved to higher country by boating time. Boulders block them from the canyon below Scorpion Rapid, so for the last 20 miles the air is much fresher. Other than this, the canyon is incredibly beautiful. The bare orange cliffs contrast sharply with the lush green vegetation along the river bottom. Sheer walls often jut straight up from the river and overhang in several places. Almost every side canyon is interesting; beautiful camp spots abound.

One of the difficult aspects of boating on the Escalante is finding a time when there is sufficient water. Many years it's not boatable at all; when it is, it's usually only boatable for a few days to maybe two weeks. In some years, such as 1983, it's runnable for a month. Rarely high enough for a raft, inflatable canoes or kayaks are probably the best way to go as they are easier to pack out. Next best is a regular kayak.

Call the National Park Service at (801) 826-4315 or the BLM at (801) 826-4291 in Escalante for flow information. You'll need about 10 inches of water on the gage at the Calf Creek bridge as a minimum. This gage is only a rough estimate, since side streams coming in at Boulder Creek and The Gulch greatly affect the flow.

The river starts out small and fairly smooth but almost doubles in size at Boulder Creek, where there are several rocky drops. The Gulch can also add a fair amount of water. The smoothest water is approximately from The Gulch to Twenty-five Mile Wash. An old cabin is up Silver Falls Creek about a quarter mile, and another cabin is at the mouth of the first side canyon on the right below Harris Wash. Below East Moody Creek are a couple of rocky drops and several wide, shallow places.

Scorpion Gulch is nice for hiking. About a half mile below here is a little rapid that leads into Scorpion Rapid, which you can't miss. The river appears totally blocked by boulders, but there is a way through on the far right. From here to Stevens Canyon, you'll encounter boulders almost everywhere. One section is too narrow to get a kayak through, but it's only a short walk around. The gradient isn't too steep, so even though the river is very rocky, the difficulty is only Class 2+.

From Stevens Canyon to Coyote Gulch, the river is wide, slow, and shallow. Coyote Gulch is hard to see until you're right there. Lake Powell backs to here when full.

At Coyote Gulch the hardest part of the trip begins—getting out. You basically have four options: (1) The easiest is to pay someone with a power boat to pick you up. This can be arranged with a marina but is very expensive. (2) Paddle on the lake for about 60 miles to the nearest marina. (3) Paddle 21 miles on the lake to Hole in the Rock and climb up this steep boulder pile to where a four-wheel-drive road comes in. (4) Hike out 3 miles from Coyote Gulch through Crack in the Wall to the dirt road on Forty Mile Ridge.

I will describe the last option, since it's the one I've done. It took two of us about 7 hours and half gallon of water each plus some drinks brought partway down by our shuttle driver. We carried one person's boat and gear about a quarter mile at a time and then went back and got the other. This gave us frequent short rests as we walked back.

From the take-out point, go about a quarter mile up Coyote Gulch. A makeshift ladder allows you to get above the first cliff. Follow the trail you'll see. It stays fairly level for a ways and then angles back and up the steep sand hill above. This is probably the worst part. From the top of the hill, Crack in the Wall is visible; it's where the sand reaches highest on the cliff way above you and has a crack angling down from left to right.

A trail leads to the crack, but it is hard to follow at times. The first part of the crack is too narrow for boats or gear. It opens on a ledge about 15 feet up where you can hand gear up. The second half of the crack is bigger but still isn't big enough for a canoe. A canoe would have to be hauled up about 40 feet with a rope. From the top you get an incredible view of Escalante Canyon.

The parking area is still two miles away across some slickrock and sand, and the cars are just over a hill out of sight. You can tell the spot by the sandy remains of an old jeep trail going up the hill in the distance.

One other problem with this run is drinking water. The main river is fairly muddy and not potable without treating. We found several springs and often got water from the smaller side canyons that had boulders blocking cattle from going up. We didn't treat the water and were fine, but later learned we were lucky. It is definitely recommended that you treat it some way.

Neil Kahn punches through a small hole on an exploratory run of Ferron Creek.
Gary Nichols.

Ferron Creek

Difficulty: Class 2 to 3 with a little Class 4.
Length: 4.5 miles.
Time of Year: Late May to mid-June.
Average Gradient: 72 ft./mi.
Flow Levels: Normal high is 450–500 cfs; record is 4,180 cfs, 27 August 1952. The gage is 1.8 miles upstream from Dry Wash, just above the reservoir.
Topo Maps: Ferron, Flagstaff Peak, Ferron Canyon.
Access: Paved and dirt road off highway 10 at the town of Ferron.
First Run: Neil Kahn, Gary Nichols–8 May 1985.

58

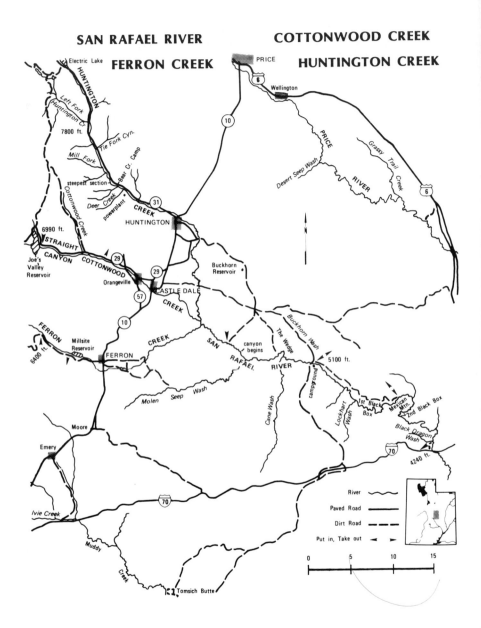

SAN RAFAEL RIVER   COTTONWOOD CREEK
FERRON CREEK   HUNTINGTON CREEK

Electric Lake

PRICE

Wellington

HUNTINGTON

Left Fork (Huntington C.)

7800 ft.

Tie Fork Cyn.

Mill Fork

Bear Cr. Camp

steepest section

Deer Creek

powerplant

CREEK

HUNTINGTON

6990 ft.

STRAIGHT

Joe's Valley Reservoir

CANYON   COTTONWOOD

Orangeville

CASTLE DALE

CREEK

PRICE

RIVER

Grassy Trail Creek

Desert Seep Wash

Buckhorn Reservoir

FERRON

Millsite Reservoir

6400 ft.

FERRON

CREEK

SAN

RAFAEL

RIVER

canyon begins

Buckhorn Wash

The Wedge

5100 ft.

campground

Molen   Seep   Wash

Cane Wash

Lockhart Wash

1st Black Box

2nd Black Box

Mexican Mtn.

Moore

Emery

Ivie Creek

Black Dragon Wash

4240 ft.

Muddy

Creek

Tomsich Butte

	River	〜〜〜
	Paved Road	———
	Dirt Road	– – –
	Put in, Take out	◄ ►

0   5   10   15

This is the farthest south of the three main tributaries that form the San Rafael River. It seems to be the smallest of the three. To get there, turn off Highway 10 in the town of Ferron at Canyon Road. Follow this up past Millsite Reservoir.

The best run is from where the road leaves Ferron Creek down to the reservoir. There is a campground near the upper end. It's about a 4½-mile run, almost all of which can be seen from the road.

The upper part has the most logs. There weren't any all the way across as of this writing, but several blocked most of the river and some forced the river to make sharp, 90-degree turns. After the campground the river has fewer trees and is mainly Class 1 and 2. It becomes rockier and steeper around Birch Creek with an occasional tree blocking part of the river. The hardest and steepest section (Class 3 to 3+) is the bottom half mile from a little above the National Forest entrance sign down to the gage, which is right above the reservoir.

Fremont River

Difficulty: Upper section, Class 3 to 6; lower section, Class 2 to 3. Small, rocky, trees, waterfalls, steep, too small for rafts.
Length: Upper section is 9 miles; lower section is the same but can be shorter or longer depending on where you put in and take out.
Time of Year: Dam-controlled, but usually highest in March, April, and sometimes May.
Average Gradient: Upper section, 130 ft./mi. (200 ft./mi. from Carcass Creek to mouth of canyon); lower section, 55 ft./mi.
Flow Levels: Normal peak is around 200 cfs with a record of 8,800 cfs on 24 July 1984.
Topo Maps: Torrey, Fruita.
Access: U-24.
First Run: Lane Johnson and Gary Nichols, lower section, 16 March 1983; upper section, 17 March 1983.

TORREY (HICKMAN BRIDGE) TO CAMPGROUND

This is an incredible section of river because of its difficulty, remoteness, and fantastic scenery. This stretch is only about 9 miles long but requires a full day to run as scouting and portaging are involved. In fact, it's probably a better hike than river run. The swift current carries you through a nightmare of rocks, and no amount of finesse or paddling skill can keep you from banging into, scraping over, and wrapping

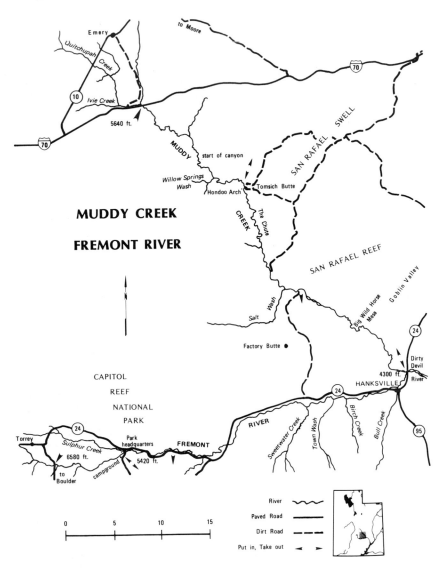

MUDDY CREEK

FREMONT RIVER

around a few of them, even if you were to scout every inch of the river. Either your kayak had better be nearly indestructible or you'd better walk much of it.

Put in at the Hickman Bridge southeast of Torrey. In less than a quarter mile the river starts dropping steeply, and dodging rocks is re-

The Dirty Devil River is the easiest path for exploring this vast canyon country. Gary Nichols.

Dave Hildebrand crashes through the best rapid on the North Fork of the Duchesne River in the Uinta Mountains. Gary Nichols.

When there's enough water, the Escalante River is one of the most scenic water-ways in America. Elvin Asay enjoys a view of Stevens Arch. Gary Nichols.

The author finds the Fremont River to be small, steep, and technical. Lane Johnson.

Triplet Falls in Lodore Canyon of the Green River brings out smiles and yells from this half-submerged paddle crew. Bill Barnes.

Snow and difficult drops, such as Hangover Falls, made us wonder what we were doing exploring the Fremont River in March. Lane Johnson.

Labyrinth Canyon of the Green River is one of the most outstanding beginning canoe runs in the state. Kirk Nichols.

quired. An occasional tree may block the way. There was one strand of barbed wire across the river about a half mile from the bridge, but we were able to fit underneath. After about a mile comes a sharp right, then a sharp left, and then an island that splits the river. This section is very rocky and should be scouted and probably walked.

The canyon begins to narrow in about another mile. The gradient steepens and several islands cut the flow in half and block the view of what's coming up. From here on you proceed from eddy to eddy, always keeping a place to stop in sight. If you can't, get out and scout. In one such spot, while scouting, I found some petroglyphs. Just below this is an island with a shallow, rocky channel on the left and a rocky, 6-foot falls on the right. A short portage on the right gets you around this.

Shortly afterward the canyon reaches its narrowest point. Some steep, rocky drops here should be scouted because it's critical to stop again before what we call Hangover Falls. Here the river makes a sharp left and then cuts right and drops 10 to 15 vertical feet in about the same horizontal distance. Above all this is a huge overhanging boulder. This is a potentially runnable rapid (Class 6), but a vertical pin is a real possibility.

Right after this is a 15-foot vertical waterfall, followed by several more steep drops and falls. The portaging is difficult. A quarter mile of paddling below all this brings you to another portage around a staircase falls hidden around a blind turn with a log across. Be careful! Check out the next drop below this before putting in again.

Not far after this the canyon opens up a little and becomes less steep. However, overhanging brush narrows the river in a few spots. Although it was all clean when I ran it, a log could easily get caught in here. The canyon opens into a little valley at the campground near the Capitol Reef National Park headquarters.

CAMPGROUND TO WATERFALL

This is a beautiful area in the heart of Capitol Reef National Park. Unfortunately, the road (U-24) follows the river. The campground and picnic area for the park are right next to the river about a mile from the visitors center. Both places are good put-in spots, or you can put in almost anywhere along the main road. It's about 7 miles from the campground to a waterfall that's visible from the road, 1.8 miles inside the east entrance to the park. The river can be run below the falls but soon becomes very slow and spread out.

Unfortunately the river is rarely runnable because of its small flow. Even in the best of conditions you'll find it hard to avoid every rock. Most of the rapids are small and rocky, often requiring tight maneuvering. One undercut spot just above a bridge is visible from the road and should probably be scouted.

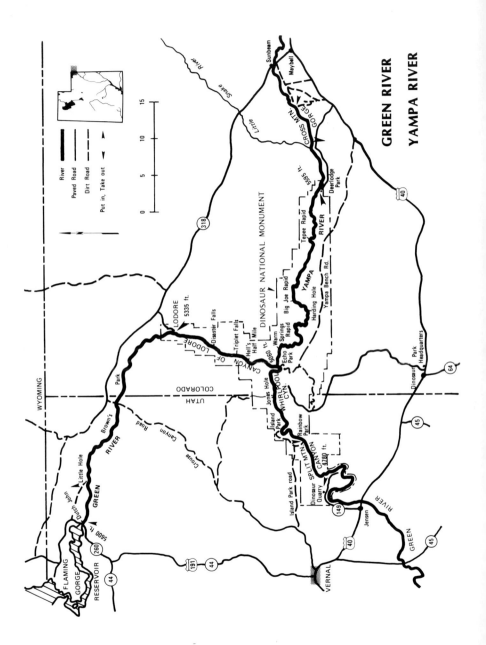

GREEN RIVER
YAMPA RIVER

Green River

FLAMING GORGE TO LODORE

Difficulty: Class 1 and 2 to Brown's Park, and flat water thereafter. Rocky when low.

Length: 7 miles from the dam to Little Hole; 46 miles from the dam to Lodore Ranger Station.

Time of Year: June, July, and August are usually best.

Average Gradient: 10.5 ft./mi. between the dam and Red Creek Rapid; 4 ft./mi. from Red Creek Rapid to the Lodore Ranger Station.

Flow Levels: This varies directly with dam releases. It is usually lower in the morning and higher in the afternoon. The peak is normally about 4,000 cfs, with a record of 19,600 cfs on 12 June 1957.

Topo Maps: Dutch John, Goslin Mountain, Clay Basin, Warren Draw, Swallow Canyon, Lodore School.

Access: U-260 and C-318.

First Run: William H. Ashley, May 1824.

One of the most popular short float trips in Utah is through Red Canyon just below Flaming Gorge Dam. The road to the river comes down from the east side of the dam. Parking is limited at the put-in, and the many rafts available for rent at Dutch John and numerous fishermen in the area make this a busy place. Launch as quickly as possible to make room for others.

There are several moderate rapids on the 7-mile run to Little Hole. Trout fishing is good, and a hiking trail follows the east side of the river to the Little Hole Campground.

Four miles below Little Hole is Red Creek Rapid, which is rockier and more difficult than any of those above. After 2 miles of river you leave the quartzite walls of Red Canyon and enter Brown's Park. Another 2.5 miles bring you to a BLM boat ramp on the left.

Eight more miles of mostly slow water bring you to Swallow Canyon where a BLM boat ramp is at the mouth of the canyon on the left. The river then crosses into Colorado 2 miles below the boat ramp.

After leaving Flaming Gorge National Wildlife Refuge, the river flows slowly through Brown's Park National Wildlife Refuge, an area named for Baptiste Brown, a Canadian trapper who moved there in 1827 after having trouble up north. Camping is allowed at designated river campgrounds.

Brown's Park, or Brown's Hole as it was originally known, was a refuge for outlaws and rustlers into the 1900s. Infamous men such as Butch Cassidy and the Wild Bunch, Isom Dart, Jesse Ewing, Joe Tolliver, Tom Horn, Mike Flynn, and Matt Rush frequented Brown's Park, and many met their death there.

The river enters Dinosaur National Park 1.5 miles above the Lodore Ranger Station. A permit is required for floating below the boat ramp at the ranger station.

Books: *River Runners' Guide to Dinosaur National Monument and Vicinity*, by Philip Hayes and George Simmons (Powell Society); *Dinosaur River Guide*, by Laura Evans and Buzz Belknap (Westwater Books).

LODORE THROUGH SPLIT MOUNTAIN TO US-40

Difficulty: Class 2 and 3, with a little 4−.

Length: 44 miles.

Time of Year: Runnable most of the year, with the peak in late May or early June.

Average Gradient: 16 ft./mi. in Canyon of Lodore; 20 ft./mi. through Split Mountain.

Flow Levels: The gage is 6.5 miles northeast of Jensen, Utah. Average high is 18,000 cfs, with a record of 36,500 cfs on 16 June 1957. This includes flow from the Yampa. For Lodore flow see Flaming Gorge flows.

Topo Map: Dinosaur National Monument, Colorado-Utah, 1966. Canyon of Lodore North, Canyon of Lodore South, Jones Hole, Stantz Reservoir, Island Park, Split Mountain, Dinosaur Quarry.

Access: The shuttle takes about 3 hours and can be done either of two ways. A back road out of Vernal crossing over Diamond Mountain is about a 50-mile trip. The road is paved partway and is fairly wide and in good shape until you reach the east side of the mountain; here it gets very narrow in a couple of spots. A rickety old bridge crossing the Green River lists its weight capacity in numbers of sheep and cattle instead of tons. When you reach C-318, head south and turn off at the road to the Lodore launching area. The longer but easier route is to head east from Vernal on US-40. Take C-318 and head northwest past the town of Sunbeam until you come to the turnoff to the Lodore Ranger Station. The take-out is at the dinosaur quarry campground, north of Jensen.

First Run: William H. Ashley, May 1824.

Dinosaur National Monument has some excellent river running on the Green and Yampa rivers. Many commercial companies operate here, though, and private permits can be difficult to get. For permit information, contact: River Ranger, Dinosaur National Monument, P.O. Box 210, Dinosaur, Colorado 81610; phone (303) 374-2216. Your application will be put into a lottery. Don't be surprised if you get a letter saying you're number 867 on the waiting list. It's worth trying for, and if you are flexible as to when you can go and can leave on short notice, you just might get a permit.

A trip through the entire length of the Canyon of Lodore, Whirlpool Canyon, and Split Mountain takes three days or more. Day trips through Split Mountain are possible, and, in fact, permits are easier to get for this.

The Canyon of Lodore is about 19 miles long and opens up into Echo Park. The rapids here are frequent and probably the best of any on the Green River, especially at the rare times when the river is high. Three of the most interesting are Disaster Falls, Triplet Falls, and Hell's Half-Mile. During spring runoff, the Yampa River greatly enlarges the Green as you enter Echo Park, where you can cool off in Whispering Cave or look at some interesting petroglyphs.

After Echo Park comes Whirlpool Canyon. The rapids aren't as frequent, but there are some good ones. Jones Hole is halfway through the canyon on the right, and is a popular camping spot, with a good hike to some petroglyphs. Friendly skunks will probably greet you or at least visit you during the night.

Island Park and Rainbow Park will give you plenty of slow water (8 miles) to relax on if the rapids have been too much for you. Then comes Split Mountain, where the river seemingly took the hard way, cutting straight through the mountain instead of going around it. Here the river picks up speed and takes you through 8 miles of good rapids before the take-out at Split Mountain Campground near the dinosaur quarry. The best rapids (Class 3) are Moonshine, S.O.B., Schoolboy, and Inglesby.

Day trips through Split Mountain start at the Rainbow Park boat ramp, which is accessible by way of the road going over Diamond Mountain.

Below the campground, the river has some riffles and small rapids for 2 or 3 miles and then it flattens out until Desolation Canyon. It takes 3 to 6 hours to go from the campground to US-40, depending on flow and how hard you paddle.

Books: *River Runners' Guide to Dinosaur National Monument and Vicinity*, by Philip Hayes and George Simmons (Powell Society); *Dinosaur River Guide*, by Laura Evans and Buzz Belknap (Westwater Books).

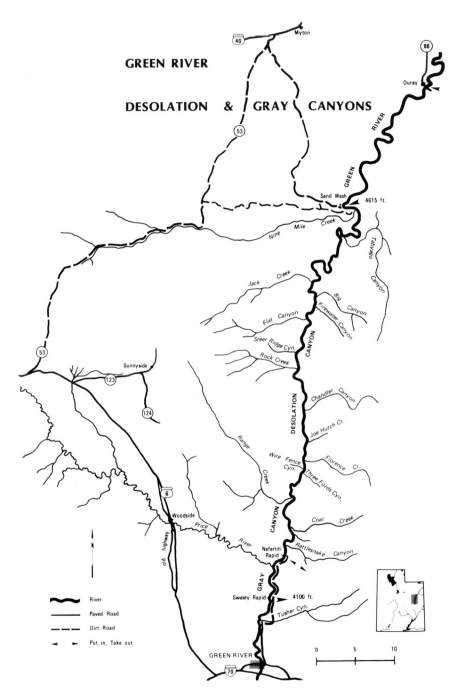

GREEN RIVER

DESOLATION & GRAY CANYONS

DESOLATION AND GRAY CANYONS

Difficulty: Class 1 to 3.

Length: 95 miles from Sand Wash to Green River, Utah.

Time of Year: Year-round, but is highest in late May or early June. A BLM permit is required for Desolation Canyon.

Average Gradient: 1 ft./mi. before Jack Creek; 6.5 ft./mi. thereafter.

Flow Levels: The gage is on the river just above the railroad bridge at Green River State Park in Green River. Average high is 19,000 cfs, with a record of 68,100 cfs on 27 June 1917.

Topo Maps: Nutters Hole, Firewater Canyon, Flat Canyon, Range Creek, Gunnison Butte.

Access: Put in off US-40 at Ouray or Sand Wash, and take out off I-70 at Swasey Beach or Green River State Park. To get to the put-in turn off US-40 just west of Myton. A BLM sign marks this as the road to Sand Wash. This road is paved for a short way and then becomes dirt. To take out at Swasey Beach or Nefertiti Rapid, go east out of Green River, cross the bridge, and take the first paved road on the left. Follow this for 6 miles and turn right on a dirt road just before a fence and cattle guard. Follow this 4 miles to Swasey Beach or another 9 miles to Nefertiti Rapid.

First Run: Powell Party, June 1869.

The Green River winds out of the Uinta Basin and enters the Tavaput Plateau, creating a gorge that splits the plateau into its east and west halves. This gorge has been known as Desolation Canyon and the lower 36 miles as Gray Canyon (not Gray's Canyon) since John Wesley Powell and his men traversed it in 1869 and 1871.

Below Ouray, as the canyon walls begin to rise, the river wanders slowly at first (but the mosquitoes are fast and numerous). Most boating parties put in another 32 miles below Ouray at the BLM ranger station at the mouth of Sand Wash. A BLM permit is required below here. Contact: Bureau of Land Management, Price Resource Area, P.O. Drawer AB, Price, Utah 84501; phone (801) 637-4584.

You get to Sand Wash by taking a 40-mile stretch of dirt road that leaves US-40 near the town of Myton. Watch the sky for rain; the last 9 miles are often in a dry streambed that could flood.

Sand Wash was the site of a ferry crossing that was active for about thirty years from 1920 into the 1950s. A sunken ferry boat can be seen at most water levels about a quarter mile below the launching area on the west side of the river. A few old buildings and a stone marker commemorating the Powell voyages and noting the entrance into Desolation Canyon are scattered among the tamarisk trees near the launching area.

The river flows peacefully for the next 26 miles, giving most people plenty of time to acquire painful sunburns if they don't cover up. Small riffles can be found at the mouths of Tabyago Canyon, Rock House Canyon, and Little Rock House Canyon.

Starting about a mile above Tabyago Canyon, the Uintah and Ouray Indian Reservation borders the east side of the river for the next 62 miles to the mouth of Coal Creek. Points of interest along this stretch include an old boat with an iron bow left under a cliff just upstream from the lower Gold Hole. Up a side canyon, but visible from the river below Stampede Flat, is a 40-foot tower capped by a balancing rock. At the western edge of Peter's Point and on the west side of the river where three canyons enter are petroglyphs of several different animals. A mile below these three canyons is a large window or arch high on the western wall. Another mile or so down, and also on the right, is Light House or Totem Rock. Through the rest of Desolation Canyon below Jack Creek, expect a rapid of varying but increasing difficulty every mile or half mile.

A mile below Jack Creek, a canyon enters on the right, a large mushroom-shaped rock with petroglyphs sitting at its mouth. Also watch the left wall as it rounds the point. A foot trail is propped up with logs where the bank becomes a sheer wall. The mouth of Firewater Canyon contains, along with a lot of bleaching cattle bones, a stone Indian granary. Nearby is a spring, and under a ledge is a sturdy house with an old bed, a stove, and a wooden door with a beveled glass window. These are best left alone.

The best-known and largest panel of Fremont-style petroglyphs in this canyon is on the right just upstream from Flat Canyon.

Rock Creek is the cold, clear stream coming from the 10,000-foot-high ridge of the western Tavaput Plateau. The canyon is over 5,000 feet deep here. Drinking water should be taken a distance upstream and still purified. Do not bathe in the stream. No camping is allowed near the stream. If you hike a few miles up Rock Creek, several large panels of petroglyphs can be found along the north side. South of Rock Creek is private land with several old stone ranch houses built near the turn of the century by Dan and Bill Seamounton.

Chandler Creek, another cold, clear stream that drains the East Tavaput Plateau, runs year-round out of a beautiful canyon 7 miles below Rock Creek. A four-wheel-drive road follows the bottom of the canyon to the river and then on to Florence Creek. There are petroglyphs on the boulders below the cliffs at the mouth of the canyon. The initials "D.J.," thought to be those of Denis Julien, a French trapper who traveled these canyons in the 1830s, are inscribed on one of the larger boulders. Also, a stone chimney from a house thought to have been built by Joe Hutch, an early settler, stands alongside the stream.

The rapids at Chandler Creek, Joe Hutch Canyon, and Joe Hutch Creek are the most difficult so far. About a mile below Joe Hutch Creek on the east are the Florence Creek Lodge and the McPherson Ranch. In

High water at Short Canyon Rapid in Gray Canyon of the Green River tosses the author around. Kirk Nichols.

1942, the U.S. Government bought the McPherson Ranch from the Wilcox family to add to the Indian reservation. Then the Florence Creek Lodge was built, which now blocks the view of the ranch.

Partway up Florence Creek are several Indian granaries and petroglyphs. A spring behind the ranch and a clear creek are the last chances for good water before reaching Green River. The widening of the canyon here marks the end of Desolation Canyon and the beginning of Gray Canyon.

After the wide valley of the McPherson Ranch, the Green River starts cutting through the older rocks of the Paleocene Epoch and the Cretaceous Period to rocks that are over 90 million years old at the mouth of Gray Canyon. Just where Gray Canyon starts is vague, but the Wire Fence area is often regarded as its boundary, since this is where the Flagstaff limestone first comes up to river level.

The rapids in Gray Canyon are separated by longer stretches of flat water, but generally the drops are steeper and longer, starting right out with McPherson's or Three Fords Rapid. As one travels deeper into Gray Canyon, the beaches that were frequently found in Desolation Canyon become rarer, so don't pass up a good site as evening approaches. In the evening and early morning, keep an eye out for bighorn sheep among the cliffs and along the river bottom.

Coal Creek Rapid is one of the rockiest rapids in these two canyons and can be scouted from the right shore. This rapid often gives an unusual forewarning of its approach—the sulphurous odor of seeps near the creek carried upriver on the breeze. Below this rocky rapid on the left are the ruins of several stone houses left from an attempt to dam the Green River between the cliffs here in 1911.

At the top of Nefertiti Rapid is a river access point on the east bank where the dirt road from Green River ends. This is the first possible take-out. Another 2 miles below, the Price River enters from the west. Petroglyphs can be found near both the Nefertiti area and the mouth of the Price River.

Five more good rapids are encountered below the Price River and above Swasey Beach, the most popular take-out for this trip. They are Butler, Sand Knolls, Stone House, Short Canyon, and Swasey rapids. Should you decide to float to the town of Green River, be warned that there is a diversion dam with tricky hydraulics and a concrete, boulder-strewn rapid (Tusher or Pumphouse Rapid) 3 miles below Swasey Beach, after which follow 8 miles of flat water to Green River State Park.

The section from Nefertiti to Swasey is a popular day run for all types of craft. Open canoeists, even if fairly experienced, should be aware that they are likely to tip over and therefore should know how to rescue themselves and others with them.

Books: *River Runners' Guide to the Canyons of the Green and Colorado Rivers: Desolation and Gray Canyons,* by Felix Mutschter (Powell Society); *Desolation River Guide,* by Laura Evans and Buzz Belknap (Westwater Books).

GREEN RIVER STATE PARK TO CONFLUENCE WITH THE COLORADO RIVER

Unless you go on Memorial Day weekend, when the annual "Friendship Cruise" is held, this is a relaxing and beautiful run. Then hundreds of powerboats roar down to the Confluence and back up the Colorado to Moab. Otherwise, I think it's about the finest beginning canoe/camping trip in the state. Plan on at least three full days in high water and four days in low water. It can be done in less, but that wouldn't give you time to hike and see the many interesting sights. The river is almost all smooth. There are a few waves about 5 miles down, shortly after the geyser, and several riffles in low water in the first 12 miles.

An excellent map of this section is found in Bill and Buzz Belknap's *Canyonlands River Guide* (Westwater Books). Get the waterproof edition and take it with you. Another excellent book is *River Runners' Guide to Canyonlands National Park and Vicinity,* by Felix Mutschler (Powell Society).

Crystal Geyser, the first attraction you encounter, is on the left 4.5 miles from the put-in. The rock is discolored by minerals from a cold-water geyser that was created by an unsuccessful test well drilled in 1936. Escaping carbon dioxide causes the irregular eruptions several times a day. The highest I've seen it go is about 60 feet, lasting as long as 15 minutes. Sometimes it just bubbles up and overflows without shooting high in the air.

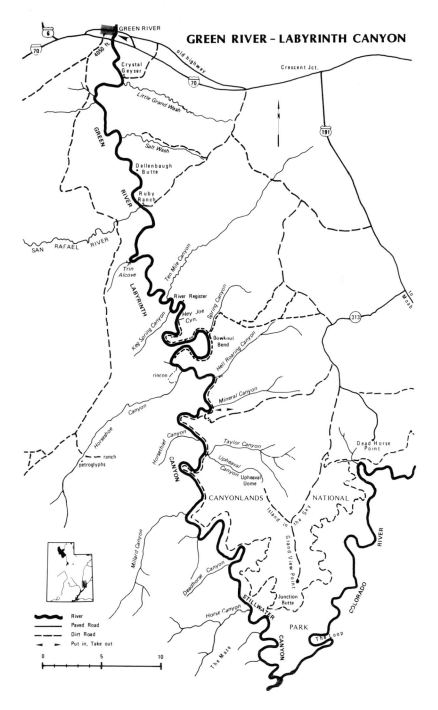

GREEN RIVER - LABYRINTH CANYON

GREEN RIVER

Crystal Geyser

Crescent Jct.

old highway

4050 ft

Little Grand Wash

GREEN

Salt Wash

Dellenbaugh Butte

RIVER

Ruby Ranch

SAN RAFAEL RIVER

Trin Alcove

LABYRINTH

Ten Mile Canyon

River Register

Spring Canyon

Hey Joe Cyn.

Key Spring Canyon

Bowknot Bend

Hell Roaring Canyon

rincon

Mineral Canyon

Canyon

Horseshoe

Horsethief Canyon

CANYON

Taylor Canyon

Upheaval Canyon

Upheaval Dome

ranch petroglyphs

Dead Horse Point

CANYONLANDS   NATIONAL

Island in the Sky

RIVER

Millard Canyon

Grand View Point

COLORADO

Deadhorse Canyon

Junction Butte

STILLWATER

Horse Canyon

PARK

CANYON

The Loop

The Maze

to Moab

River
Paved Road
Dirt Road
Put in, Take out

0   5   10

Denis Julien, a French trapper, carved his name in several places along the Green and Colorado rivers. This one is about 200 yards from the Green River up Hell Roaring Canyon. Gary Nichols.

Dellenbaugh's Butte (The Anvil or Inkwell) is 19 miles along on the left, and the San Rafael River comes in 4 miles beyond that across from Ruby Ranch. You can drive to Ruby Ranch and launch, but you may have to pay a fee for the privilege. The entrance to Labyrinth Canyon is about 5 miles beyond Ruby Ranch. Bull Bottom is here on the right with an interesting trail up the cliff to the top. Trin Alcove (Three Mile Canyon) is 2 miles beyond, with canyons nice for hiking. Watch out for rattlesnakes, however.

Seven more miles downstream are some petroglyphs on the left a short distance upstream from an island. A trail to the top is just below them. The river register is not far beyond this—about 6 miles. There are some interesting carvings here, but don't add to them. The inscriptions early explorers made are unique; yours aren't. A Denis Julien inscription ''16 Mai 1836'' located 3 miles beyond the register on the left just above the high-water mark is difficult to see. Julien was a French trapper in the area. The ''Launch Marguerite 1909'' inscription (from an early river trip) is also on the left about a mile away. A dirt road follows the river along this stretch. Coming in at Spring Canyon, it goes up and down the river to several mines.

The saddle at Bowknot Bend is reached in another 3 miles. Although there's room to camp here, the mosquitoes are usually bad. A short, steep hike up the rockslide to the ridge lets you see the river on both sides. There are also many names carved in the rocks on the saddle. If you feel you must add your name, do it on a rock that's loose on the ground and stack it with others you'll find. Don't write on the cliffs. As you go around the bow you'll see several mines and an old ore bucket still hanging from a cable across the river. A couple mines just

Crystal Geyser, only 100 feet from the Green River, is a cold water geyser that erupts at irregular intervals when carbon dioxide builds up enough pressure. Eruptions vary from a few feet to over 60 feet. Kirk Nichols.

recently stopped operating as the demand for uranium has gone down. A trail on the other side of the saddle goes to the ridge from Oak Bottom.

On the right 3 miles past Oak Bottom and just past Horseshoe Canyon is a 1914 inscription that includes some names of a U.S. Reclamation Service survey crew. Similar inscriptions may be seen at Bowknot Bend and near the lower D. Julien inscription. His lower inscription, dated "1863 3 Mai," can be seen along with some drawings 200 hundred yards up Hell Roaring Canyon. A road follows the river from here to the most common take-out at the end of Mineral Bottom, approximately 68 miles from the put-in.

This area is dry and barren except along the river, so don't plan on finding fresh sidestreams coming in for drinking water. Bring your own. Good camping spots can be hard to find in high water because of the dense tamarisk. Usually the upper and lower ends of a "bottom" are better than the middle. In lower water there are many more camp spots on beaches and islands.

I haven't run below the take-out at Mineral Bottom, but the river continues much as it did above: slow and meandering. You will enter Canyonlands National Park about 5 miles beyond. Labyrinth Canyon ends about 15 miles distant, and then you enter Stillwater Canyon. You will pass an old cabin, several ruins, cliff dwellings, and also Upheaval Dome.

If you run this section, you will need a means of getting out at the Confluence—either a powerboat to go up the Colorado River to Moab, your own motor, or a permit to continue on down the river. Cataract Canyon is only 4 miles away.

Gunnison River

Difficulty: Class 2 to 4−. Far from help, drops with boulders.
Length: 14 miles.
Time of Year: Dam-controlled; can be run most of the time.
Average Gradient: 21 ft./mi. (steepest section is about 45 ft./mi.)
Flow Levels: Normal high is about 3,000 cfs, but can be run as low as 300 to 400 cfs.
Topo Maps: Red Rock Canyon, Black Ridge, Lazear.
Access: To put in from Delta, go through Olathe. Take the first left after the sign "Montrose 9 miles." This is Falcon Drive. Go 3.8 miles to the Peach Valley Road sign. Don't turn off but go straight at this sign about 1.6 miles and take the right fork. This winds back southeast then heads up the mountain and over the top. About 2.5 miles down the other side is the Chukar trailhead. The road is often rutted but doesn't usually require a four-wheel-drive vehicle. If it has rained recently, don't try it in any vehicle. This dirt road is about 10 miles long. Don't take any of the less-traveled side roads cutting off it. Any time the road forks and you can't tell which is the main road, go left.

The take-out is much simpler. About 6 miles past Austin on C-92, turn right on a dirt road with a hard-to-see BLM sign saying "Gunnison River Forks." A railroad crosses C-92 about a quarter mile beyond the turnoff, so if you get that far, go back. It's about 1 mile of good dirt road to the river.
First Run: ?

CHUKAR TRAIL TO NORTH FORK

The Gunnison is one of those rivers that dam builders think should only have current where it drops down the spillway of one dam into the lake formed behind another. Fortunately, Black Canyon, one of the deepest and narrowest gorges in the United States, is protected as a national monument. Boating through here, however, requires more portaging time than river time, but just below Black Canyon is Gunnison Gorge. Here, the violence found upstream is more subdued. There is still much of the same black rock, but the canyon is not so deep and the river is less constricted. This stretch is unprotected except by its inaccessibility and a group of people who have fought off attempts to dam this last deep canyon before the Gunnison flows into the Colorado River.

Getting to the put-in is the hardest part of this trip. Once at the Chukar trail head there is about a mile-long hike to the river. It's not as bad as it sounds—at least it's downhill. It would be an awful carry back up, however. Rafts are occasionally carried down on horseback.

The first few miles are in the black rock with Class 2 and a few Class 3 rapids. When the orange sandstone appears on the right, the river widens and slows. When you go back into the black rock the canyon narrows and you enter several miles of the best rapids. These are pool-drop and are Class 3 to 4 in difficulty depending on water level, with high water being harder. The river then begins to slow and you leave the black rock behind and enter a section with orange sandstone cliffs and then several miles of open country before the take-out where the North Fork comes in.

Gunnison Gorge is a nationally recognized trout fishery. A Colorado license is required, and a number of special regulations are enforced. Inquire locally about these.

Huntington Creek

Difficulty: Class 3 to 5. Long continuous rapids, many trees across, steep, small.
Length: 6 miles from Left Fork to Mill Fork; 6.5 miles from Mill Fork to the Utah Power and Light experimental farm just below the power plant.
Time of Year: June, sometimes May.
Average Gradient: 123 ft./mi. (Steepest stretch drops 160 feet in 0.9 miles).
Flow Levels: Normal peak is around 500 cfs with a record of 2,500 cfs on 2 or 3 August 1930.
Topo Maps: Candland Mountain, Hiawatha, Red Point, Rilda Canyon.
Access: U-31.
First Run: Lane Johnson and Gary Nichols, 23 June 1984.

This is a steep mountain stream, one of the more difficult rivers in the state. Several nice camping places are available along the creek. A road following alongside makes much of it easy to scout. However, some of the most dangerous sections are hidden from the road. It is potentially runnable even above where the Left Fork comes in (some portages required) and has fast current clear through the canyon and out to U-10 near Huntington.

The upper part is mainly Class 3 and 4 but is filled with trees, making it extremely dangerous. Every bit of this, at least down to the Utah Power and Light dam, should be walked first. The current is fast enough and a few turns sharp enough that you can't see some of the logs until it's too late to stop. You must know where to get out ahead of time.

If you put in at the next bridge below Mill Fork you'll miss most of the logs, but you still need to scout ahead. If you put in at Mill Fork, there are a couple of dangerous logjams and a steep boulder drop. After this the creek is a fairly constant Class 3 to 4 and a thrilling run until you come to a slow, winding section that catches a lot of the fallen trees.

Below this park-like area the river goes smoothly away from the road. Just out of sight, you start to plunge down a steeper gradient through more difficult drops and suddenly you're in the hardest rapids on the river (Class 5−). This lasts for about a half mile and then eases to Class 4. In less than a mile the river has dropped 160 feet. This section, called the Crooked Elbow, is just upstream from the Bear Creek Campground. Below this are some tight turns and large boulders, then the water backs up behind a UP&L dam that is a definite portage.

Below the dam is almost a mile of excellent Class 4 rapids. The river then eases as the canyon opens and the river turns away from the road and heads toward a big power plant on the hill. When the river gets to the hill it turns left. A fence crosses the river here with chain and pipes hanging down to catch debris. The left side was broken and I got through, but this could be dangerous; it's hard to see until you're right there.

As the creek cuts back to the road, it becomes more channeled and eases to Class 2 to 3. Still swift, it enters farmland from here on. I've only gone as far as the UP&L experimental farm. Below there, the water is diverted in a couple of places and has a few sections that look like they become more difficult again for a short distance.

FERRON CREEK   **HUNTINGTON CREEK**

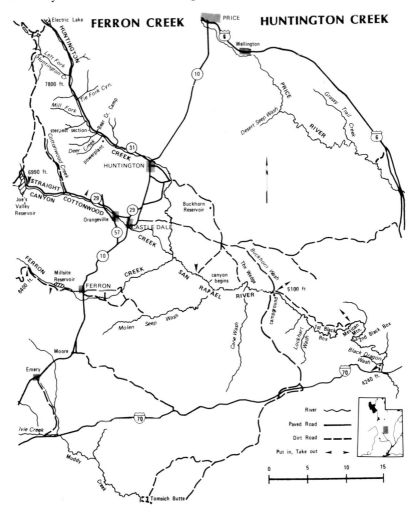

JORDAN RIVER

BIG & LITTLE COTTONWOOD CREEKS

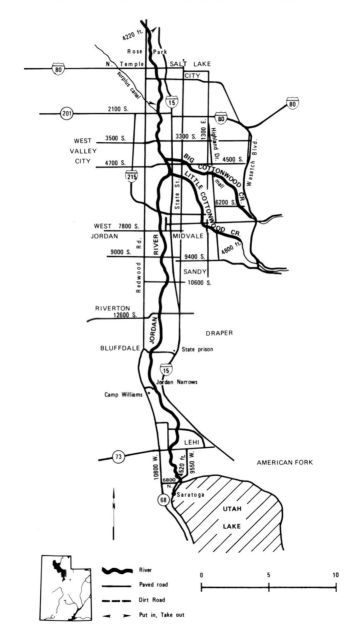

Jordan River

Difficulty: Class 1 and 2 plus several dangerous low bridges and barbed-wire fences. Mostly slow and flat except for the Narrows.
Length: 10 miles from Utah Lake to the Narrows; 5 miles for the Narrows; 11 miles from Bluffdale to 7800 South; 11 miles from 7800 South to 2100 South; 8 miles from 1700 South to Rose Park.
Time of Year: Much of it can be run year-round, but overall it is highest in early spring before irrigation begins.
Average Gradient: The Narrows drops as much as 30 ft./mi. in places; most of the rest of the river drops only a few ft./mi.
Flow Levels: Average peak is around 800 cfs, but this varies from section to section because of diversions. After 2100 South the average is about 150 cfs.
Topo Maps: Saratoga Springs, Jordan Narrows, Midvale, Salt Lake City South, Salt Lake City North, Farmington.
Access: Roads cross at many points along the route.
First Run: ?

For many years the Jordan has been a much-maligned river. People have awful pictures in their minds of a slimy, rat-infested open sewer with numerous dead-sheep eddies. Actually, it's quite beautiful in most sections, and people are usually surprised at how nice it can be when they first go down.

Much work has been done to clean up the Jordan, and it is looking nicer every year. There are still a number of spots that need improving, and though it's not a river to swim in, it makes for some very enjoyable canoeing. Occasionally small rafts and rowboats are used. The State Parks and Recreation Division, along with some cities along the river's route, are developing the Jordan River Parkway. They are putting in parks, trails, and docking areas, with the eventual goal of having a green belt along the river's entire length. At present, the main developed area runs from 1700 South to 1200 North. Several canoe and kayak races are held there each year. South of 2100 South dredging operations may change some of the descriptions below and may mar the beauty and naturalness of the shoreline. Also, a great deal of concrete was dumped along the edge where high water eroded the bank. These cement blocks are sharp and some have rebar sticking out. Beware!

Two new, dangerous dams have been built on the Jordan River. One is on the Narrows and replaces the canal crossover. The other replaces the old dam just above 9000 South. Even if the gates are open, offset cement pillars block the way.

UTAH LAKE TO THE NARROWS

Easy access is available where the river exits Utah Lake near Saratoga. From there to the Narrows Pumping Station is 10 miles (3–4 hours) of easy and mostly slow water. A few roads cross this section, including 8600 North (U-73) and 9600 North. The river constricts as it approaches the Narrows, steep hills on both sides replacing the open river bottom.

THE NARROWS

Just north of Camp Williams on Redwood Road, a sign that reads "Jordan Narrows Pumping Station" marks the road that goes down to the Narrows. At the pumping station, the river splits into three channels; the center one is the actual river and the side ones are irrigation channels. You will have to paddle across the river above the dam and portage to where you want to put in. The river becomes much swifter here.

A number of things have changed through here since the first edition of this guide. A higher footbridge finally replaced the lower one, which was then washed out by high water in 1983 and 1984. The railroad bridge that was between the dam and the low footbridge was also destroyed. It has been replaced, but the debris from the old bridge is now in the water creating a dam and steep drop full of concrete reinforcing bar. If the water is extremely high it can be run but should be scouted at any level. This is only about 150 feet below the pumping station dam.

In about 1.5 miles you'll come to a train trestle. Be careful that you don't get wrapped around the pilings. The next obstacle is a small diversion dam that normally must be walked around. The diversion channel on the right is an irrigation ditch that will create a problem farther downstream. It will be contained in a concrete channel that crosses over the river to the left side. Unfortunately, there's little or no clearance underneath. Just before you get there the river makes a sharp left and a pipe comes in on the right from the irrigation channel. Get out and scout. The river will start bending right and then straighten. At this point, if you look carefully, you will see the top of a cement tower that is part of the canal crossover. Immediately after a turn to the right, a wall all the way across the river will confront you. A small eddy whirls on the right a few feet before the wall. The eroding bank is causing the eddy to slowly disappear.

Less than a quarter mile farther downstream is an arched bridge. The river narrows a little afterwards and there are a couple of nice sets of rapids. In high water these waves are big. Watch out for overhanging trees and branches.

About 3 miles from the pumping station there used to be a fairly large diversion dam. High water has destroyed part of it. On the right side a small road comes in from the road between Bluffdale and the state prison. It's a good access point. From here to the Bluffdale Road the river is still swift with some small waves. Watch out for barbed-wire fences crossing the river.

The Narrows is *not* for beginners. The water is swift, there are low bridges and dams, overhanging trees and bushes, and a fair amount of maneuvering is required. Normally it can only be run when the farmers aren't irrigating. In high-water years it may be runnable all the time, but usually it can't be run after about 1 May. Make sure there's still water in the river at Bluffdale before attempting it. Often there is plenty of water at the Narrows Pumping Station, but it's all diverted below at the smaller dam, possibly drying the main river completely. Allow about 2 hours to run this stretch.

BLUFFDALE ROAD TO 7800 SOUTH

This section is about 11 miles long, running mostly through peaceful farmland. Allow 3 hours for the run. Several roads can be used for access: Bluffdale Road, 12600 South, 10400 South, 9000 South, and 7800 South. North of the Riverton Road (12600 South) there aren't any barbed-wire fences as of this writing. There was a diversion dam between Bluffdale and 12600 South, a second one just after 12600 South, and a third just before 9000 South. High water has destroyed or gone around all of them; however, they may be rebuilt. A low, yellow pipe between 9000 South and 7800 South requires ducking or getting out if the river is fairly high. Presently, the high water has cut a new channel that bypasses this.

7800 SOUTH TO 2100 SOUTH

This 11-mile section can be run year-round and takes 3 to 4 hours to do. During irrigating season, enough water seeps back and comes in from other streams to make it boatable. Right under the 7800 South bridge, the river drops through some cement blocks, creating a small rapid. Sometimes this gets blocked with trees, so be careful.

The river has a fast current, with a few riffles and small drops but mostly smooth water. At 6400 South there is a narrow bridge with cement supports in the water. Several canoes have wrapped around this bridge, with one death resulting, so be careful. Immediately below the bridge was a small curling wave all the way across the river. At very high flows this wave becomes huge and is more of a hole. It has been a fun place for kayakers to play and do endos. It's also been the site of two hole-riding contests. Unfortunately, it changed in 1984 and isn't quite as easy to play in. Now that the river is dropping, it has turned into a steep, dangerous, almost vertical falls.

Between 4800 South and 4500 South was a diversion dam that could usually be run by ducking under some metal framework. High water has buried the diversion dam, and I'm not sure what is still hiding under the water there.

By 3500 South the river is slow. Just before 2100 South you go under the freeway. At 2100 South the river goes over a barely noticeable diversion dam where part of the river becomes a surplus canal. Get out at the cement dock here and carry across 2100 South. The actual river goes under the road through several pipes and goes more directly north than the surplus canal.

1700 SOUTH TO ROSE PARK

It's about 5 miles from 2100 South to the Fairgrounds and just over 3 more to where Redwood Road crosses the river. This takes about 3 hours to run. This is the first area being developed as part of the Jordan River Parkway. You'll find numerous parks, jogging and equestrian trails, exercise courses, and other developments along here. The park and launching ramps on both sides of the bridge at 1700 South are part of this project. This section is slow but really beautiful, with many overhanging trees and several developed parks. The International Peace Gardens directly adjoining the river at about 1000 South are well worth visiting and make a nice lunch spot. There is a dock and park at 800 South and another dock just north of 300 South that can be reached from a side street. At about South Temple, you'll encounter a diversion dam for the Utah Power and Light plant. A canoe flume has been built there, supposedly easing the drop for boaters.

The Fairgrounds has a large cement docking area. Right after this is a dock at the Northwest Multipurpose Center, and there are other docks at 1000 North and 1200 North. Just before the river goes under Redwood Road, you pass through the Rose Park Golf Course.

Lake Fork

Difficulty: Class 2 to 4+. Steep, narrow, rocky, logs, probably too small for rafts.

Length: Upper section, 1.6 miles; lower section, 6.7 miles.

Time of Year: June, and sometimes late May and early July.

Average Gradient: Upper section, 144 ft./mi.; lower section, 62 ft./mi.

Flow Levels: Normal high is about 800 cfs with a record of 2,180 cfs on 19 June 1940. Lake Fork reached 2,140 cfs on 22 June 1983.

Topo Maps: Lake Fork Mountain, Mountain Home.

Access: Paved and dirt roads off US-40 (see map).

First Run: Upper—Lane Johnson, 4 July 1984; Lower—Les Jones, 30 June 1974. Les also ran some above Moon Lake on 20 May 1974.

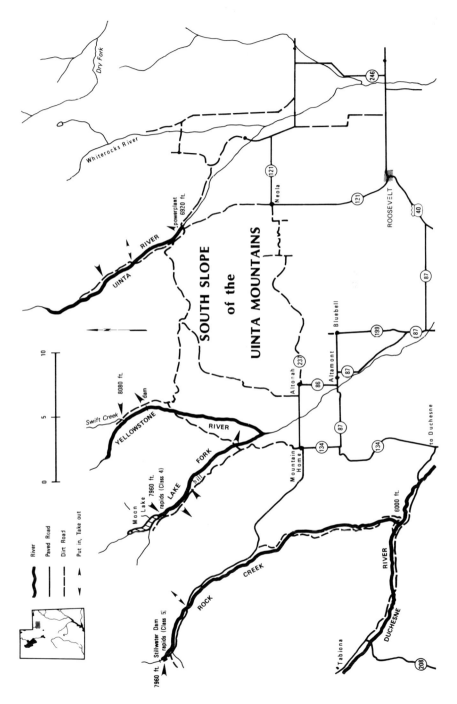

Below Moon Lake, Lake Fork has some excellent whitewater for about 1.5 miles. The first quarter mile is class 2+ to 3 with some fairly tight maneuvering and good gradient but no major drops. Just above the gage, the river swings right and makes some short drops through boulders and then funnels into a narrow, clean, 4-foot drop. You may want to scout this, as all this happens in a short space and can catch you unaware.

There is a relatively flat section after this for a hundred yards. The gage is near the end just above the river's biggest drop (Class 4+). This is wider, rockier, and steeper than the drop above and should be scouted. A dirt road comes down to the gage, where there's a good camping area.

The third best rapid comes up just after a straight bouldery section. The river cuts sharply left and narrows down. This is longer than the other two but doesn't drop as suddenly. All three rapids are in the Class 4 to 4+ range.

The rapids ease up a little but are still continuous and rocky, mainly Class 3 and some 2. A diversion dam puts water into the Farnsworth Canal, and you'll have to get out. A road comes into here from the main road just above two old collapsed log cabins and below Raspberry Draw. Below the diversion, the river is smaller and spreads out with the channel blocked by a maze of fallen trees.

If you go down the road about two miles or so—below the beaver ponds but above the big hill on the east side of the road—you can put in again. The short road to the river isn't marked and is seldom used. It cuts back up the canyon slightly. Topographical maps show Lake Fork Corral here. The first 1.5 miles is Class 1 and quite pretty. Once past the cliffs on the right, there is one rapid after another, with slight breaks in between, all the way to the bridge. One of the first is undercut on the right as it makes a sharp left turn. The rapids through here are Class 2 to 3+ depending on water level.

The banks through this lower section are bushy, making it difficult to stop at high flows. The river also splits into smaller channels in several places. The potential for logjams is great, but most trees get caught in the slow section above. Take out at the bridge where the road going to Yellowstone River crosses.

Little Cottonwood Creek

Map: See page 82.
Difficulty: Class 1 to 3+. Dangerous dams, low bridges, trees.
Length: 7 miles.
Time of Year: Late May to early June.
Average Gradient: 72 ft./mi.
Flow Levels: Normal high is around 300 cfs with a record of 1135 cfs on 26 September 1982.
Topo Maps: Sugar House, SLC South, Draper.
Access: Many city streets.
First Run: Bob Cooper, Spring 1973.

Yes, there is some interesting boating right in Salt Lake Valley. Like Big Cottonwood Creek, this stream is best known where it drops steeply from ski resorts down through a beautiful glacier-carved canyon. The gradient (300+ ft./mi.) is too great for boating, but Little Cottonwood becomes manageable after entering the valley. It's best to run it before peak runoff rather than after, since the streambed is usually cleaned out before runoff. Peak flows bring in new rocks, logs, and other debris.

There is a dam at the Willow Creek Country Club and below it, for about a quarter mile, the river cascades over several cement energy dissipaters. Put in below them. Two men in a raft tried to run these in 1983 and were killed. A dirt road off Creek Road takes you to just below these energy dissipaters. It appears that several more are being installed so you may have to put in at Creek Road.

The river is swift until about 900 East. There are many diversion dams; some are runnable, some are not. Scout all bridges and drops where you can't see what's below. One spot in particular is potentially bad because it's hard to see until it's almost too late to stop. This is behind the "castle" house just above 1300 East. A cement wall is on the left and the river bends right. You can barely see a headgate before it's too late to stop. The river makes a very sharp right, hits a cement wall, and makes a steep drop of about 6 feet. Another bad spot, but easier to stop above, is just below 1300 East where the creek makes a sudden 5-foot drop.

Much of the section below 1300 East until just past I-215 has recently been confined between gabion walls. About a block after going under 7000 South, the river turns right and then, as it cuts sharply left, a rapid starts and continues to the triple tunnel that carries Little Cottonwood Creek across I-215. The center tunnel is the main one; 100 feet after leaving the tunnel is a short, slanting drop.

Shortly after 6400 South are three barbed-wire fences in a row about a hundred feet apart. Just above 900 East are some interesting drops and cement chutes. Make sure they're clear before running. At Murray Park, you won't be able to fit under most of the bridges. You can fit under State Street if it's clear at flows up to about 375 cfs.

Immediately after going under I-15 you have to get out because two low pipes block the way. You'll get an exciting ride through the single tunnel under the railroad and then over a diversion not too far after. You should scout these and decide whether you can run them. Little Cottonwood Creek flows into the Jordan River just above 4800 South.

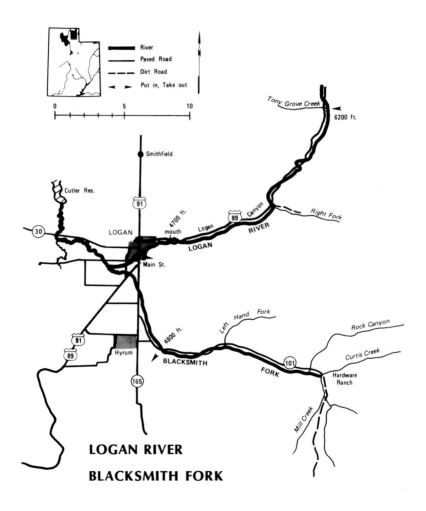

LOGAN RIVER

BLACKSMITH FORK

Logan River

Difficulty: Class 2 to 5−. Continuous rapids, rocky, brushy banks, steep. Mostly too small for rafts.

Length: Ricks Spring to Preston Valley Campground, 8 miles; lower canyon, 1.5 miles.

Time of Year: Mid-May through June.

Average Gradient: Ricks Spring to Preston Valley Campground, 82 ft./mi.; lower 1.5 miles in Logan Canyon, 133 ft./mi.; through town, 47 ft./mi.

Flow Levels: Average peak is about 1,000 cfs with a record high of 2,000 cfs on 21 March 1916.

Topo Maps: Tony Grove, Temple Peak, Mount Elmer, Logan Peak, Logan.

Access: US-89 follows the river in the canyon.

First Run: ?

LOGAN CANYON SECTION

This is a clear, fast-dropping mountain stream in beautiful Logan Canyon. Since the road follows the river, you can put in and take out wherever you want. Scouting is also easy.

In high water it's possible to put in as high as the Tony Grove turnoff at about milepost 394. Most of the time Ricks Spring just past milepost 390 is a better put-in, plus the spring itself is interesting. This section is fairly constant Class 2 to 3+ with few eddies. About a quarter mile from the spring is a rocky drop we call the Slippery Slide. Four miles further is the hardest rapid in this section, about a quarter mile above where the road crosses the river (about ¾ of a mile above milepost 385). A big boulder blocks the middle of the river and then comes a short, steep drop with several rocks just under the surface that you need to avoid. Some good waves follow. The road is right next to the river here, so it's easy to scout.

The river continues swift and rocky, past where the Right Fork joins, to below Preston Valley Campground, where it eases a bit.

About 4 miles of Class 1 plus a few rocky spots bring you to a dam. Several low bridges to cabin sites go through here. There's about a mile of river between this dam and a second dam.

You can put in for the lower section just below the second dam, but you will have to get out above a low footbridge a half mile down. It's easier to simply put in below the footbridge (just above milepost 376). Below it is a steep, slanting drop off a diversion dam. It's runnable on the right when the water level is right. Scout it first. From here down, don't expect much rest. It's constant Class 3 to 4+ (some Class 5 at really high water) for almost 2 miles with only tiny eddies for stopping. This whole section should be scouted. Just above where the road crosses the river and on through a couple of drops below the bridge is the hardest section, with several holes that can easily stop your boat.

The Logan River should be run with care. A tree could easily fall across it, and the numerous small trees and bushes that overhang the river can act as strainers. There aren't a lot of tall trees along the sides, so it's less likely than some rivers to have logjams—but it only takes one. Scout it thoroughly.

MOUTH OF LOGAN CANYON TO MAIN STREET

This is a pretty run for an urban river. Some areas are lined with cottonwood trees that completely canopy the river, and there are many beautiful homes. The run takes about an hour, medium water level being the safest. Overhanging bushes make stopping difficult in high water.

Three drops need to be planned for. The first one is easy to see—a good-sized diversion dam that drops about 15 feet. There's a footbridge right above it, so land on the right in the canal and portage. The next drop is under a bridge and has nice waves but is easily runnable. The third drop is harder to see but has a good landing on the right in someone's backyard (respect their property). The drop can usually be sneaked. Most of it is a nasty hole.

The river becomes more overgrown after the third drop as you near Main Street. Below Main Street is even worse and the current continues swift until after the next road crossing.

Muddy Creek

Difficulty: Class 1 to 3. Small, rocky, far from help.
Length: 71 miles from I-70 to Hanksville (about 3 days).
Time of Year: May or early June.
Average Gradient: 19 ft./mi.
Flow Levels: Normal peak is about 150–300 cfs with a record of 9,400 cfs on 5 September 1981. The logjam you float under in the narrow section indicates that this record was surpassed before the gage was installed.
Topo Maps: Mesa Butte, Emery 1 SE, Emery 4 NE, Wild Horse Mesa, Factory Butte, Hanksville.
Access: I-70, U-24, and dirt roads.
First Run: Whole section from I-70 down—Ed Gertler and Gary Nichols, 28–30 May 1983. Tomsich Butte to mines—Cal and Mike Giddings, Les Jones, Bill Staude, Jim Byrne, J. Dewell, 3–4 May 1975. (Much of this was walked because of low water. Les Jones, Cal, Mike, Omana, and Steve Giddings went again on 10 May 1975 and had enough water to run it.)

Muddy Creek is a truly outstanding desert river. It is seldom run, mostly because it is seldom runnable. The canyon is very dry with virtually no springs or side streams unless it's raining, and there is very little wildlife. The river is well named; it's extremely muddy. But the incredible scenery, isolation, and numerous rapids make up for all this.

There is a gage on the left bank about 200 yards downstream from the I-70 bridge (the bridge is at about milepost 98). You'll need a minimum of about 2.3 feet on the gage to avoid a lot of scraping. Sections have been run (walked?) when much lower. If you can't find a stick gage by the round metal shack, then you have plenty of water (assuming it hasn't washed away). The gage only goes to 3.0 feet.

The water is swift with many Class 1 to 3 rocky rapids that prove fairly tricky for an open canoe. You will probably see some cattle for a while. A gage and then Lone Tree Crossing are at about mile 10. The river then slows, entering a narrower canyon as it drops into the Navajo Sandstone. Watch out for a barbed-wire fence shortly after entering the canyon. The many sand waves liven things up through here. Willow Springs Wash is large and comes in on the right, one map calling it Mussentuchit (Mustn't Touch It) Wash.

The Wingate Sandstone soon rises above the river, and then you come to Tomsich Butte at about mile 28. A dirt road comes in to some old cabins and mines and is where some groups put in. Hondoo Arch is

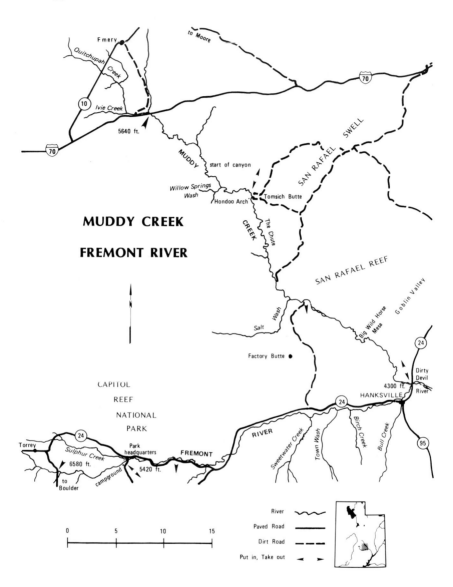

MUDDY CREEK

FREMONT RIVER

about a mile below here on the right. Another barbed-wire fence was near here.

The river again picks up speed and has more rapids. It cuts through a deep reddish layer (Moenkopi Formation) into a harder, lighter-colored, and smoother cliff layer (Cutler Formation). A good rapid after a sharp right turn leads you into a narrow canyon in this rock layer. This lasts about a half mile and then the cliff drops down until you go around a bend and then rises again, forming a narrow box canyon for the next 3 or 4 miles. This area which maps call The Chute is extremely beautiful and rather eerie: You're in a narrow, swift (Class 1) corridor of wall-to-wall water. In some places 300-foot cliffs overhang so you can't see the sky, and it is occasionally so narrow you can't turn a kayak sideways. Near the end of this section the canyon narrows to about 7 feet wide at river level and is even narrower about 20 feet up where flash floods have left a logjam that you paddle under.

After coming out of this box canyon, the rapids are almost continuous for a couple of miles. After a particularly good rapid some partially hidden old buildings are encountered. The road from Tomsich Butte comes in here, making this a possible take-out.

You're now about to rise through all the rock layers you've dropped through since leaving I-70. These layers all drop sharply as you cut through the San Rafael Reef. You're through the reef at about mile 47, where the river slows and widens greatly. In about 1.5 miles a dirt road comes in on the right making another nice take-out.

From here it's almost 22 more miles to the confluence with the Fremont River and the bridge by Hanksville. While most of this is open, barren land, there is a shallow canyon near Big Wild Horse Mesa, from about mile 56 to 62. The bridge is at about mile 71.

This is fragile country. It takes a long time for plants you kill to grow back, and trash and waste doesn't decay in such a dry area. So take care. Very few people have been through here, so much of it is almost untouched wilderness. Please don't leave any trace of your passage.

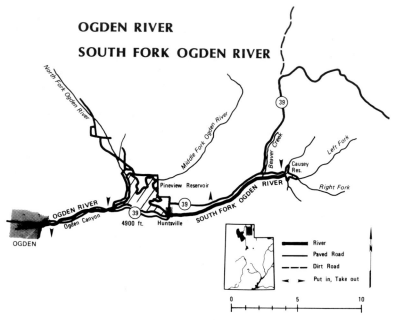

Ogden River

Difficulty: Canyon section, Class 2 to 5. Steep, rocky, continuous, probably too tight for rafts. South Fork, Class 1 to 2, with one 3+ rapid.

Length: Canyon section, 5 miles; South Fork, 7 miles.

Time of Year: Usually May and early June; dam-controlled.

Average Gradient: Canyon section, 80 ft./mi. (bottom part is 148 ft./mi.); South Fork, 54 ft./mi.

Flow Levels: There is no gage, but from my observation, the normal high for the canyon section is about 600 cfs. The highest I've seen is 1,300 cfs, and it's flooding cabins at this stage. For the South Fork, the normal high is 800 cfs with a record of 1,890 cfs on 3 May 1952. It reached 1,660 cfs on 16 May 1984.

Topo Maps: Huntsville, North Ogden, Ogden, Brown's Hole, Causey Dam.

Access: U-39 follows most of it.

First Run: Ogden Canyon—Bill Burton and Mike Mutek, Spring 1974. South Fork—Gary Nichols, 13 June 1984.

*Lake Fork spills out of Moon Lake and drops through a beautiful alpine canyon.
Few sections of river are this gentle.* Gary Nichols.

The author is dwarfed by the sheer walls of The Chute, a narrow box canyon cut by Muddy Creek. Ed Gertler.

Brian Seeholzer drops back for more after an endo at the Jordan River hole riding contest. Steve Becker and John Armstrong.

The bottom 2 miles of Logan Canyon offer few places for the author to rest. Kirk Nichols.

The Provo River, only an hour from Salt Lake City, is a favorite spot for river runners in small craft. Jeff Stevens takes his turn at a slalom race. Kirk Nichols.

DAM TO MOUTH OF CANYON

Most of this run can be scouted from the road. The bottom two miles should be carefully scouted. The upper part is fairly easy—Class 1 and 2. A low footbridge to some cabins can't be seen from the road, but it is fairly easy to see in advance from the river. A little farther on, three cables hang across the river about 100 feet apart and are easy to fit under except at flood stage. At high water you'll find a number of good surfing waves.

Partway through the canyon is a gas station from where you can scout the bridge behind it. There's a permanent-looking log underwater on the upstream side. This causes a small pour-over under the bridge that occasionally traps debris.

Below the gas station the river becomes steeper with several Class 2+ to 3 rapids (Class 3 to 4 at flood stage) and they are more continuous. Some big waves develop through here in flood stage. Once the cabins on the right disappear (there's a large turnout in the road just above this), the river drops very steeply through the rest of the canyon. In high water it's Class 5+ and almost impossible to stop. At medium high levels it's Class 4 to 4+. It becomes very rocky at lower levels.

Just below the mouth of the canyon the river bank is heavily wooded, fallen trees often blocking the river. The bridge by the restaurant here is a good take-out.

SOUTH FORK OF THE OGDEN RIVER

The South Fork is small and boatable for a short time each spring. It's about a 7-mile run if you put in below Causey Reservoir at County Memorial Park and take out at the mouth of the canyon. But since a road follows it, you can have a run of whatever length you want. There are several campgrounds along the river, and a gage is visible from the road about halfway through the run. Above 3.0 feet is best.

About 1.5 miles below the dam, Beaver Creek enters adding a fair amount of water in the spring. Most of the river is swift with many Class 1 and a few Class 2 rapids. Rocks aren't too numerous, but there are enough, along with logs, that you'll do a fair amount of maneuvering. Occasionally a tree falls all the way across. A small runnable diversion dam can be seen from the road.

The most difficult stretch is a rocky, steep, Class 3+ section near the mouth of the canyon. It's on an "S" turn and is fairly long, the bottom part easily seen from the road. The upper part, which is hardest, is partially blocked from view by trees and bushes.

About a mile below the rapid, a paved road turns off the main road and goes to an old bridge and a diversion dam. The river is slow here and it is a good place to take out.

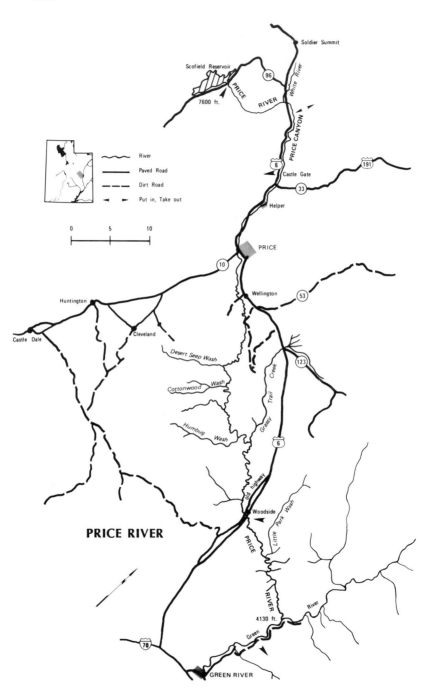

PRICE RIVER

Price River

SCOFIELD RESERVOIR THROUGH PRICE CANYON

Difficulty: Scofield Reservoir section, Class 1 to 3; Price Canyon section, Class 3 to 5. Steep, rocky, continuous, diversion dams, trees.

Length: 11 miles from Scofield Reservoir to US-6; 4 miles more to the picnic area access, 8.5 miles more to Castle Gate, 4.5 miles more to Helper.

Time of Year: Dam-controlled; usually May or June.

Average Gradient: Scofield section, 38 ft./mi.; Price Canyon section, 96 ft./mi.

Flow Levels: No gage; best when fairly high.

Topo Maps: Colton, Kyune, Standardville, Helper.

Access: US-6 and U-96.

First Run: Scofield section—Cal Giddings and Roger Turnes, 10 September 1972; Price Canyon section—John Johnson and Jeff Niermeyer, Spring 1978.

SCOFIELD RESERVOIR TO PICNIC AREA AT TOP OF PRICE CANYON

The first mile is fairly flat with logs possible all the way across, then there are a few small rapids between flat stretches. A railroad follows the canyon. When the tracks cross from the left to the right and the canyon narrows, there are several good Class 2 rapids until the tracks cross back to the left, the best rapid lying underneath this last bridge. After a footbridge come several more good rapids. Watch for a small white fence on the left coming from the railroad tracks. There is a smooth wire across the river here followed by another good rapid about a quarter mile below.

The best rapids for this section are in a mile-long stretch cutting through a cottonwood grove. Watch out for logs. Just after entering the cottonwood section, the railroad crosses again to the right side of the river. As the cottonwoods end, another barbed-wire fence crosses.

When the canyon opens up there is a steel cable hanging across the river. Shortly after this, you enter the last narrow canyon, the one you see from US-6. The river is fast and smooth until you come to a couple of small rapids under the highway. In another 4 miles of meandering you reach the take-out.

Brian Smoot enjoys the nonstop action of the Price River in Price Canyon. Dave Hildebrand.

PRICE CANYON

This section is steep, continuous, and rocky (Class 3 to 5−), requiring great control at all times. There are very few calm pools to recover in, and the eddies are small. The riverbed is unnatural in most places because of a railroad on one side and the highway on the other, so expect some very sharp rocks.

At the top of Price Canyon, above Helper, is a picnic area where a road leads to the river. It's the take-out for the upper run. Around the first bend is the first rapid. If you can't handle it, you'd better stop here because it gets much harder. After about a hundred yards the river calms down, then progressively builds up to Class 3 and 4. In medium-low water you may want to walk around a couple of rocky drops. Some look clean from above but really aren't.

Be sure to scout as much of the run as you can. I've had to pull trees out that had fallen across the river. One hidden below a drop was too large to move. A few drops and a couple of diversion dams along the way may need to be portaged.

A good place to take out is at about milepost 228. A boarded-up mine and a large turnout on the west side of the highway (right side when facing down canyon) make a good place to leave your car. Just below here is Castle Gate.

I don't really recommend the section below Castle Gate. The river still has some excellent boating, but the coal mining area begins here and it's often ugly. There are also many diversions.

If you do continue, just below milepost 228 is a small but easily runnable drop. Shortly afterwards comes a diversion dam with cement sides and a walkway across that you will have to portage. The next drop is shortly after, right at Castle Gate, where the canyon narrows. This drop can be seen from the road and is just above the water treatment plant. Portage this also.

Below here is fairly constant Class 2 to 3− with a few slightly harder spots. You go under a bridge as the river cuts left. After the river turns right, a small shack is visible on the left side at another diversion. This is right behind the water tank. I was able to run the right side. For almost 2 miles afterward, there are no more dams, but there is one low footbridge I had to brace way over on my side to fit under. The next diversion dam is broken and has a runnable slot in the middle.

Not far below here is the most dangerous dam. It's actually a double drop immediately after a bridge. The river drops about 6 feet and then in a few feet drops again about 3 more. This can be seen from the road. Like many dams on the Price, this one is especially hazardous because even if the reversals don't get you, reinforced concrete and sharp metal pieces probably will. The water is slow right above this double drop, and it's possible to paddle under the bridge above it and catch an eddy on the right about 5 feet before the drop. It's a short, easy portage from here.

Below the double falls are some nice waves and then you come to another dam. This looks runnable from the road but is full of sharp metal rails. Not far below is another unrunnable dam with about an 8-foot drop. The steep banks make the portage difficult. Below here is a good take-out bridge in Helper. I'm not sure what's below here except for the waterfall at the golf course.

WELLINGTON TO WOODSIDE*

Put-in is at 1st Street in Wellington. Within a mile there is a 5-foot dam to be portaged. Three bridges side by side are the next landmarks, one for the railroad and the other two for roads. About 3 miles from the put-in, near a coal preparation plant, is a suspension footbridge with a 2-foot dam beneath. Just around two short bends is a 10-foot unrunnable dam.

The river is mostly smooth and winding in the upper part. At first high banks and bushes partially block the view, but visibility improves as you go along.

*I haven't run this but will list what I was told by a friend, Ed Gertler, who did. His run was in very high water—8.9 feet on the gage at Woodside.

A road crosses the river 64 miles above the mouth, and a canyon forms gradually, first with rubble slopes and then a solid cliff layer. The canyon continues until several miles below Grassy Trail Creek. The rapids are frequent and sometimes long, mainly Class 1 above Grassy Trail Creek and Class 2 below. Then the canyon opens more with low bluffs and views of the Book Cliffs. The country is very empty with only occasional wildlife such as pronghorn, beaver, and ducks.

WOODSIDE TO CONFLUENCE WITH GREEN RIVER

Difficulty: Class 1 to 3. Rocky, far from help.
Length: 23 miles.
Time of Year: Usually May or June.
Average Gradient: 20 ft./mi.
Flow Levels: Normal high varies greatly due to irrigation needs and rarely exceeds 1,000 cfs. One of the largest runoff peaks was 3,430 cfs on 30 May 1983. The record is 8,500 cfs on 10 September 1961.
Topo Maps: Woodside, Cliff, Gunnison Butte.
Access: Put in where US-6 crosses the river near Woodside. Take out anywhere between the confluence with the Green River and the town of Green River.
First Run: Cal Giddings, Gary Haltmayer, Ernie Partridge, 23 June 1968.

Woodside consists of a boarded-up gas station, a couple of abandoned homes, and a tourist area where a geyser once was the big attraction when the old highway was in use. US-6 crosses the Price River here, about 36 miles southeast of Price. Upstream, under the bridge at the old highway, is a gage. The minimum for running this stretch is about 4.2 feet, approximately 400 cfs. A level of 5.5 feet makes it much easier to avoid rocks.

The river is flat and winding for about 6 miles until just before entering the canyon—about an hour of steady paddling. A dirt road coming in from Woodside goes partway down the canyon on the left.

The rapids come in groups, with fast water and smaller waves in between. Several side canyons come in creating small drops. The best whitewater starts after the jeep road crosses to the right side and leaves the river. The rapids from here to the confluence aren't really big (Class 2 to 3), but they do require lots of maneuvering and occur frequently. About a mile above the confluence is an interesting old cabin and corral.

It takes about 7 hours to get to the confluence with the Green River, high water cutting this time greatly. A dirt road coming from the town of Green River goes a little beyond where the Price River comes in, or it's another hour if you paddle to Swasey Beach. (See Green River, Gray Canyon section.)

Provo River

Difficulty: Class 1 to 4. Trees, bridges, dams. Rafts will probably have trouble above Deer Creek.

Length: Soapstone to U-35 bridge above Woodland, 7.5 miles; 18 miles more to US-40; 6 miles from Deer Creek Reservoir to the Olmstead Diversion Dam; 1.5 miles more to bridge below Bridal Veil Falls; 2.5 more to the Murdock Diversion Dam; 8 more to U-114.

Time of Year: Above Deer Creek Reservoir, May and June; Provo Canyon, May to September; below canyon, varies greatly depending on diversions above, usually May or June.

Average Gradient: Soapstone to US-40, 68 ft./mi.; Deer Creek Reservoir to Olmstead Diversion Dam, 15 ft./mi.; Bridal Veil Falls section, 100 ft./mi.; bridge to Murdock Diversion Dam, 80 ft./mi.; Murdock Diversion Dam to U-114, 36 ft./mi.

Flow Levels: Normal high above Deer Creek Reservoir is about 1,500 cfs with a record of 2,950 cfs on 28 May 1975, for the Woodland gage, and 4,020 cfs on 31 May 1983, for the Hailstone gage. The normal high below Deer Creek Reservoir is about 600 cfs with a record of 2,260 cfs on 3 June 1983.

Topo Maps: Above Deer Creek Reservoir—Soapstone, Woodland, Francis, Heber City. Below Deer Creek Reservoir—Aspen Grove, Bridal Veil Falls, Orem, Provo.

Access: U-150, U-35, US-189, city streets in Orem and Provo, U-114.

First Run: Deer Creek Reservoir to Olstead Diversion Dam—Cal Giddings, 1959; Bridal Veil section—Cal Giddings and Gary Haltmayer, 14 July 1968; Section below Bridal Veil—Cal Giddings and Ernie Partridge, 15 June 1968; Les Jones and Bruce Lium did the section below Woodland to US-40 in June 1957. Other sections, including above Soapstone, were done at different times, mostly between 1972 and 1976 by Les Jones along with various others such as Cal Giddings, Jim Byrne, Reed Jensen, and Roger Turnes.

SOAPSTONE TO US-40 (HAILSTONE JUNCTION)

From Soapstone, along U-150, until about a half mile below where the North Fork comes in, is mainly Class 2 with an occasional log problem. Below here the river swings away from the highway and you enter Pine Valley. The logjams through here are terrible. The river sort of splits into two halves, and both are plugged with trees. Plan on a number of portages and be extremely careful in high water. The rapids through

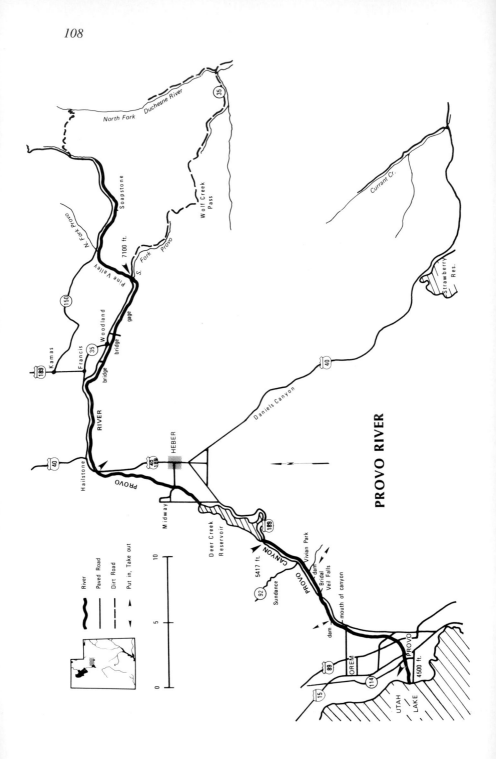

PROVO RIVER

here are generally small, and much of the land is marked "No Trespassing."

It's probably wiser to skip this section and put in where the river goes under U-35, a few miles east of Woodland. The river mainly stays in one channel and has almost constant Class 1 and 2 rapids with a few nice surfing spots. There are many summer homes along here. About 2 miles down is a gage where the river goes next to the road. A good medium-high level is 3.0 feet on the gage, which is about 800 cfs.

The river swings left away from the road, and about halfway to the next bridge (Woodland Bridge) is a diversion dam. Its slanting, rocky drop can be run in a few spots if there's enough water, but scout it first. There is what looks like a broken diversion dam a little afterward that is easily runnable. It takes about a half hour to get to the bridge from where the river swings away from the road. To reach the next bridge takes another half hour of paddling. Unless it has been moved, a house washed in during the high water of 1984 blocks much of the river just above the bridge.

The rapids through both these sections are mainly Class 2 with an occasional log problem. In high water the river is very fast and not for beginners.

Below the bridge the Provo River continues much the same for about 10 miles to US-40. This takes two to three hours to run, most of it through farmland with cottonwood trees and willows lining the bank. The Jordanelle Dam will back water through this area. The only place that seems to have any large rocks is a section against a hillside on the left about a mile above US-40.

DEER CREEK RESERVOIR TO THE OLMSTEAD (FIRST) DIVERSION DAM

This is the most popular run on the Provo River. It follows US-189 through Provo Canyon and is about 6 miles long. The run is easy, but the water is swift and cold. It is runnable usually from May through September because of the dam. Work is being done on the road in the canyon, and it's possible that this will cause changes in the river.

Dirt roads go to the river about a quarter mile below the dam. Turn off immediately on either side of the Heber Creeper (train) overpass; both roads run together at the bottom of the hill to several good put-in spots.

Around the first right bend below the dam the river goes under a bridge. Watch out for pilings and a few waves here. A little farther down, the river splits almost equally. The right channel goes past a privately owned campground and has a small footbridge across it. The left channel had a bridge across it until the high water of 1984 washed it away; I don't know if this has been rebuilt. Watch out for these bridges if the river is really high.

There used to be a rapid about a mile from the dam called Bone Crusher, but high water in 1983 smoothed it out. The only serious hazard on this section is the Heber Creeper bridge partway through the run. The pilings are at an angle to the current, so there isn't as much room to fit through as may first appear. It is also occasionally blocked with debris. Several canoes have been wrapped here and a few people have been hurt. Watch out and portage if necessary. This bridge is visible from the road, so it's probably a good idea to scout it on the way to the put-in so that you'll recognize it when you come down in your boat.

The last part of this run, below Vivian Park, is very slow. Be sure to take out before the diversion dam. The gage that used to be above Vivian Park was washed out in 1983.

OLMSTEAD (FIRST) DIVERSION DAM TO THE MURDOCK (SECOND) DIVERSION DAM

The river looks very calm below the Olmstead Diversion Dam. It is— until you go around the first bend. Then it suddenly narrows and starts dropping quickly through a rocky area. It splits up with some sharp turns and is often blocked with logs. Scout this before running. Soon after this is a small park (Upper Falls); the river has eased up a little by then.

Some good drops (Class 2 and 3−) and fun waves follow between the park and Bridal Veil Falls. You'd better know what you're doing if you go past here. The river then drops very steeply (Class 3 to 4) past the parking lot at Bridal Veil Falls down to an island. Getting around the island can be tricky at low or really high levels. Again, be sure to scout this before running.

The river stays very white for the next several hundred yards, with one drop all the way across the river that will try hard to stop you and maybe give you a reverse pop-up. After this the river eases to Class 2 and goes under the main road.

For the next 2.5 miles to the Murdock Diversion Dam, the river is almost constant Class 2 with a few slightly harder sections. One of the best drops is at the upper end of Canyon Glen Park where the river goes under an old train trestle that is now a jogging path. This trestle is occasionally used by kayakers and swimmers as a high-level launching pad into the deep pool below it.

Watch out for logs across the river. Almost every year a few trees fall across.

MURDOCK DIVERSION DAM TO UTAH LAKE

During much of the summer this stretch is almost dry, most of the water being taken out at the diversion dam. This section primarily goes through Orem and Provo, past some very large and fancy homes. The river while still in the canyon is Class 2 becoming Class 1 after leaving the canyon. A few places are wide and shallow, but there's fairly good current all the way until just before Utah Lake. The steepest and hardest section is the first part as you're leaving Provo Canyon. Trees occasionally block the river, but the biggest and most dangerous permanent obstacles are the five diversion dams. Some can be run and some can't.

The first two dams are close together by the mouth of the canyon at the power plant, just before you come to the road that crosses the river to Orem. Both can usually be run, the first on the far left and the second on the far right. But scout both and decide for yourself if you can run them. The third dam is about a quarter mile past the road heading to Orem. It can be run on the right, but must be scouted first. The fourth dam just above a bridge about a block north of University Parkway should be portaged. There's a park and picnic pavilion just above on the right. The fifth dam immediately below a bridge where Columbia Lane crosses on Provo's west side is a bad one. Get out above the bridge and portage.

The take-out, if you want to avoid the slow water to Utah Lake, is at the bridge where U-114 crosses. The state park on Utah Lake is also a place to take out.

Rock Creek

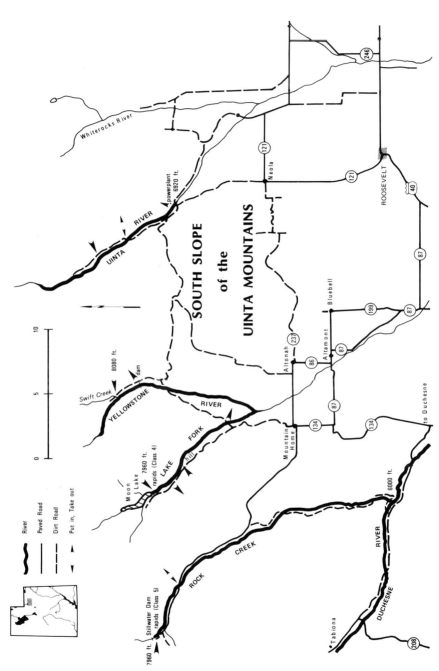

Rock Creek

Difficulty: Class 2 to 5. Steep, rocky, trees. Probably too small and rocky for rafts.
Length: The section described is 5 miles long; much more can be run.
Time of Year: June, and occasionally late May and early July.
Average Gradient: 96 ft./mi. (170 ft. in first mile).
Flow Levels: Normal high is around 1,400 cfs with a record of 2,760 cfs on 17 June 1971.
Topo Maps: Tworoose Pass, Kidney Lake, Dry Mountain.
Access: From US-40 and U-134 to Mountain Home and then paved road to the northeast along the river.
First Run: Parts by Les Jones, June 1973, and Kirk and Gary Nichols, 15 July 1983.

Rock Creek has what I feel are the two hardest runnable rapids of any river in the Uintas. The first, Class 5, is quite long; the second is Class 4 to 4+, depending on the water level.

If you put in at a gaging station below the dam, you almost immediately enter a rocky, Class 3 rapid that swings to the left. The river then makes a sharp right and slams into the undercut cliff on the left. (Unless the river is quite low, you can't tell that it's undercut.) The Class 5 rapid starts immediately after this. Scout before entering the Class 3 rapid; large boulders create steep drops and sharp turns.

The next hardest rapid comes after a short break. It's shorter and the drops aren't as great; the boulders are a little smaller, but there are more of them.

Two more rocky drops in the Class 3+ range are encountered in the next quarter mile, then comes an easier section of Class 2 and 3 for about a mile. Watch out for logs here. When these channels all come together and just below some old gage markers, there are three or four Class 3 rapids. The river then splits, but not as much as earlier. Again, watch out for fallen trees. Take out at the bridge. Below it the river slows and meanders through meadows.

A gage is available at the bridge. You'll need about 3.0 feet minimum to run this upper part without having to walk shallow areas. A good level for the run is 3.7 feet, about 600 cfs. Really high water can be very dangerous. Enjoy this run while you can. By about 1988 the Central Utah Project will dry up this river.

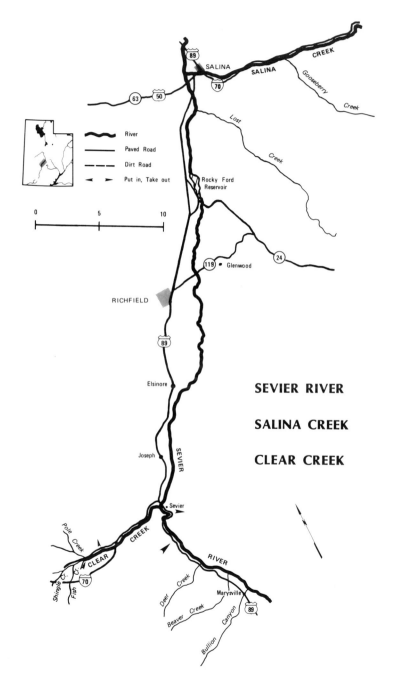

SEVIER RIVER

SALINA CREEK

CLEAR CREEK

Salina Creek

Difficulty: Class 2 to 6. Trees, tunnels, rocky drops, steep dirt banks, dams.

Length: 11 miles from I-70 exit 72 to Gooseberry Road; 8.5 more to Salina.

Time of Year: May to mid-June.

Average Gradient: 79 ft./mi. (two sections drop more than 120 ft./mi.).

Flow Levels: Normal high is 300 to 400 cfs with a record of 1,800 cfs on 26 August 1970. On 27 May 1983, the creek reached 1,400 cfs during runoff.

Topo Maps: Salina, Steve's Mountain, Water Hollow Ridge.

Access: I-70 and frontage road.

First Run: Lane Johnson and Gary Nichols, 3 June 1983; Pinball section—Neil Kahn and Gary Nichols, 8 May 1985.

Salina Creek is normally very small—you can usually jump across it. But in some years, for a short time it gets high enough to run, and in extremely rare years, such as 1983, it becomes a raging torrent and is boatable for several weeks. When Salina Creek goes way over its banks and eats away the roads, it's best to stay off; but when it's just slightly over its banks, this is a fast, exciting river.

Interstate 70 follows Salina Creek fairly closely and a frontage road follows much of it even closer. It looks like it could be run starting at exit 72 as a large side stream comes in here. I haven't run this first part, but it looks narrow and rocky in many spots with several overhanging trees and bushes. Several tunnels go under the freeway, and a drop blocked by big boulders probably needs portaging. I've run from just below here when the river was slightly over its banks, the water level used for the following description.

There is a steep, bouldery, Class 4 drop about 4 miles above the Gooseberry turnoff. The river then eases to a good, solid Class 3 for a while with a few mild spots. Two tunnels going under the freeway are fast and fairly steep with a sudden drop into back-curling waves at the end of each. Several other interesting drops and holes highlight the way.

There are also three square tunnels: one right above the Gooseberry road, one under the road, and one right after. The third tunnel has a challenging hole just before it.

About a half mile below, a stream from Gooseberry comes in and begins a long Class 3 section (very rocky in lower levels) that goes into a stretch with sheer dirt banks. Three miles below the Gooseberry turnoff is a long Class 6 rapid (Class 5 at lower flows) with Class 3 to 4 drops right above it. I call it Pinball rapid. Don't go into this narrow part without scouting and being sure you can get out above the Class 6 rapid. This is mostly hidden from the freeway by a bluff but is easily seen from the frontage road.

Below this hard rapid the river eases to Class 2 and 3 until you come to a large diversion dam that is visible from the freeway. It must be portaged. After going under the freeway there's a smaller dam. Then, in about a mile, the river turns right, away from the freeway, and heads into the town of Salina.

The San Juan River offers access to many interesting Indian ruins. Gary Nichols.

San Juan River

Difficulty: Class 1 to 3. Rocky in low water.
Length: Bluff to Mexican Hat, 28 miles; Mexican Hat to Clay Hills Crossing, 56 miles.
Time of Year: April, May, and June. Can often be run year-round in a canoe or kayak.
Average Gradient: Varies from 5 ft./mi. to almost 12 ft./mi.
Flow Levels: Normal high is 6,000 to 7,000 cfs with a record of 70,000 cfs on 10 September 1927 (before Navajo Dam). On 6 October 1911, it was probably higher, but there was no gage. The gage is on the left just above the Mexican Hat Bridge.
Topo Maps: Bluff, Boundary Butte, Mexican Hat, Goulding, Grand Gulch, Clay Hills.
Access: US-163, U-261, U-263.
First Run: E. L. Goodrige, a gold prospector, Spring 1882 (one source said 1879).

BLUFF TO CLAY HILLS CROSSING

The San Juan is a more impressive river than I expected. I've avoided it for years because I thought it would be boring, hot, and crowded. It's also far from Salt Lake City, the shuttle is long, and permits are required. Most of these problems turned out to be minor, and I didn't find it to be the least bit boring. Permits are issued for a small fee by the BLM, San Juan Resource Area Office, P.O. Box 7, Monticello, Utah 84535; phone (801) 587-2201.

We hired a shuttle driver in Bluff at Recapture Lodge. A river running company there also offers shuttles. The price paid was very reasonable and the service efficient.

The river was crowded, but this was only noticeable at campsites—not while on the river. The temperature isn't too bad if you go in the spring. July and August can be very hot and the river can get very low.

The Salt Lake City number of the National Weather Service for recorded flow information, 539-1311, gives the daily flow at Bluff. At 7,000 cfs, which this description is based on, the river is fast with very few slow areas. There are numerous rapids and almost constant small waves. Below 3,000 cfs the river is slower and easier.

The fabled sand waves weren't quite as impressive or as frequent as I'd expected, but they were still challenging. The largest we saw had a vertical height of about 4 feet, plenty big enough to swamp an open canoe loaded with gear. I suspect that reports of 10-foot sand waves are really based on the slanting length of the wave rather than true vertical height, although, who knows what 15,000 or 20,000 cfs might create.

SAN JUAN RIVER

BLUFF

47 163

4300 ft.

Sand Island
Launch

Butler Wash

Comb Ridge

Comb Wash

Chinle Creek

4 Foot Rapid

8 Foot Rapid

Ledge Rapid

Mexican Hat Rock

Turkey Rock

BLM launch ramp

Gypsum Creek Rapid

MEXICAN HAT

47

163

261

Honaker Trail

Goosenecks
Overlook

Mendenhall Loop

John's Canyon

Government Rapid

Slickhorn
Canyon

Grand
Gulch

263

Steer Gulch

Whirlwind
Draw

3700 ft.

Buckhorn
Canyon

Moonlight Creek

CLAY HILLS
BOAT RAMP

Powell
Lake

River

Paved Road

Dirt Road

Put in, Take out

If you want detailed information on geology and locations of ruins and rapids, be sure to take the following guides with you: *Geology of the Canyons of the San Juan—A River Runner's Guide,* by the Four Corners Geological Society; and *A Naturalist's San Juan River Guide,* by Stewart Aitchison.

The best Indian ruins and petroglyphs along this section are in the first 7 miles below the Sand Island bridge. Some of the best petroglyphs are on the right at mile 4.5 about a quarter mile below Butler Wash. The best cliff dwelling is at about mile 6 on the right and is hard to see from the river. Land in the willows and walk about a quarter mile across the sand flats to the cliff.

The first 9 miles are in a wide canyon with greenery contrasting with the pink Navajo Sandstone cliffs and then the darker Kayenta and Wingate cliffs (mile 6 and mile 7). The south side of the river is Navajo Indian land between Montezuma Creek and Chinle Wash. A permit from their tribal council is necessary for hiking or camping in this area. The river cuts through the Comb Ridge, and the narrow canyon starts at about mile 9.5 with an impressive cut through the Lime Ridge Anticline. Campsites can be hard to find at times below here; most are where side canyons come in.

The waves and small rapids become almost continuous from here past Four-Foot Rapid at mile 11.5 to Eight-Foot Rapid, some very exciting in an open canoe. Eight-Foot Rapid, which is at mile 17, was not as hard as it looked. Several good camping spots are nearby. I saw some wild horses while there.

Ledge Rapid is at mile 19. Mexican Hat Rock is at mile 23.5 on the right, and Turkey Rock is on the left at mile 25.9. Shortly after a BLM launching area is Gypsum Creek Rapid at mile 27. The rapid is split by an island; the left side is hardest. A half mile below is Mexican Hat Bridge, with a boat ramp on the upstream side on the right. Cold drinks, ice, and ice cream are available at the store there.

The river has fewer riffles and rapids below Mexican Hat and through the Goosenecks. The Goosenecks start with Mendenhall Loop, where a short hike to the saddle takes you to an old cabin built by Walter E. Mendenhall, a gold prospector in the 1890s. At about mile 38.5, if you look back upstream, and again around the loop at about mile 41, the Gooseneck overlook is visible high on the cliff top.

Honaker Trail is on the right at mile 44.3, with several good campsites. The hike up the trail is well worthwhile, both for the view of the canyon and to see the trail itself. When you first look at the cliffs, it's hard to believe a trail could go up them. Gold fever drove people to amazing feats.

Many rapids are encountered between the Honaker Trail and Slickhorn Gulch, especially in the area around Government Rapid.

Government Rapid, at mile 63.5, was a little easier than expected, and Slickhorn Rapid, at mile 66.3, was a little harder.

Grand Gulch comes in at mile 70.1, and camping is available above a ledge or on a beach at lower water levels. This canyon goes about 50 miles and has many Indian ruins in the upper end. Permits are required for hiking more than 3 miles from the river.

Clay Hills Crossing is at mile 83.6, the river slowing from Grand Gulch to here. When Lake Powell is at capacity, this whole stretch is on the lake. Clay Hills road is 11 miles of dirt out to U-263.

Jim Zitnik and Ralph and Claudia Henricks canoe through the famous Goose-necks of the San Juan. Gary Nichols.

San Rafael River

Difficulty: Class 1 to 5. Narrow, steep rocky drops, falls, sheer walls, far from help, probably too tight and narrow for rafts except in upper canyon.

Length: 23 miles from confluence of Huntington, Cottonwood, and Ferron creeks to the bridge by the San Rafael Campground; 22 miles more to end of first Black Box; 20 miles more to I-70.

Time of Year: May to late June.

Average Gradient: Upper section, 10 ft./mi.; first Black Box, 44 ft./mi.; second Black Box, 32 ft./mi. Individual segments much steeper.

Flow Levels: Normal high is around 800 cfs with a record of 4,630 cfs on 10 September 1980. The peak on 20 June 1983 was 3,740 cfs.

Topo Maps: Hadden Holes, Wilsonville SE, Red Plateau SW, Red Plateau SE, The Wickiup, Beckwith Peak SW, Tidwell Bottoms.

Access: U-10, I-70, and dirt roads in between.

First Run: Upper section—? First Black Box—Cal Giddings, J. Dewell, Jim Byrne, and Roger Turnes, 13–14 June 1971; Second Black Box—same group, June 1972; both boxes together—Cal and Steve Giddings, and Les Jones, early June 1978; both boxes including running the waterfall—Ed Gertler, John Johnson, and Jeff Niermeyer, 24 June 1978.

The upper San Rafael flows swiftly through open desert country until it enters an incredibly beautiful canyon cutting into the San Rafael Swell, a huge uplift that has been carved into massive buttes and twisting serpentine canyons. The San Rafael River cuts one of the most majestic of these canyons.

This river forms when three streams draining the 11,000-foot peaks of the Wasatch Plateau come together on the desert floor. During high water it is possible to put in on one of these: Ferron Creek, Cottonwood Creek, or Huntington Creek. Until they come together, expect barbed wire and logjams. The biggest danger, though, is the biting fly. Prepare to donate at least a pint of blood. After the confluence, the river widens and slows and there are fewer fences. If you want to avoid running the tributaries and the open-desert section, a small dirt road cutting off the road to The Wedge will take you to the river just before the canyon starts.

The run through this first canyon is extremely beautiful. Sheer walls overhang the river in several spots. There are no real rapids, just swift water, riffles, and a few small sand waves. Several side canyons

SAN RAFAEL RIVER
FERRON CREEK
COTTONWOOD CREEK
HUNTINGTON CREEK

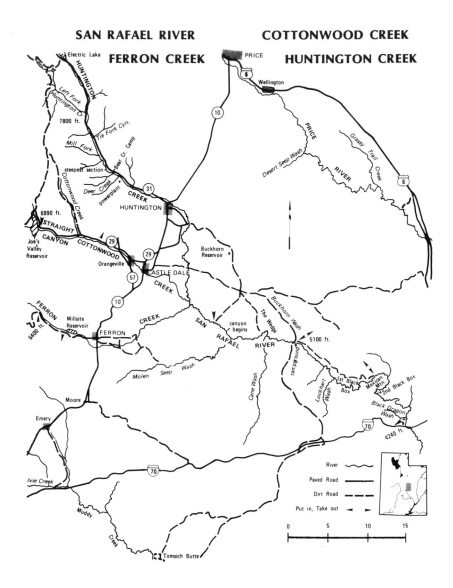

come in that make interesting hikes, and camp spots are plentiful. The canyon opens into a land of giant mesas and spires. Take out at the bridge by the San Rafael Campground, watching out for a wire fence that crosses the river about a mile above the bridge.

To get to the campground, turn off U-10 just northeast of Castle Dale on what shortly becomes a dirt road. It's about 13.5 miles to The Wedge turnoff. Go past here and straight at the next split (not left). This will take you to Buckhorn Wash and some interesting petroglyphs and pictographs. Follow the wash down to the main valley and the bridge crossing the San Rafael River. The campground is just across the river.

This bridge is a good put-in for the Black Box sections. They are extremely dangerous above 1,000 cfs. A seldom-used road on the opposite side of the river from the campground generally follows the river until the break between the two Black Boxes near Mexican Mountain. Near the end of this road you can walk to the edge of the first Black Box and look down hundreds of feet to the river. This road is about 16 miles long, and the last half mile may be washed out.

After leaving the bridge by the campground, the river goes about 10 miles before the walls close in. Then for a mile you're in a box canyon where the river runs smoothly between sheer walls, the beginning of the first Black Box. About where Lockhart Box enters, the rapids begin and the walls aren't quite so sheer. The rapids start out easily but soon increase in difficulty and frequency. There are several miles of Class 2 with a few Class 3 drops. Many are long and much maneuvering is required. The rapids then change character into short, steep drops of almost Class 4 difficulty. You cross a couple like this then come to a place where you can't see over the edge of a drop. Scouting reveals that the river disappears into a narrow crack and drops 15 feet. This must be portaged.

From here down, the rapids are fairly short Class 3 and 4 boulder drops. The canyon narrows and vertical cliffs rise straight out of the water again. Land on the left above a 12-foot waterfall and scout. Most of the water goes right and disappears down a crack between the wall and the giant boulder filling the canyon bottom. The only run is on the left, twisting through narrow slots to the brink of the falls and dropping 12 feet into the pool below. If you are boating on less than about 450 cfs, there won't be enough water on the left side and you'll have to climb down where the waterfall would be.

There are several more steep, narrow, twisting drops below here, all of which can and should be scouted. Finally you come out of the Black Box into a wider canyon going around Mexican Mountain. The dirt side road comes in here on the left, making a possible take-out or put-in.

As you go around Mexican Mountain, the river is smooth with a few small rapids; 5.5 miles of this type of water brings you to the second Black Box. This is even narrower than the first. The water goes smoothly around a bend to the left and then as it turns right you go under Swasey's Leap. Supposedly Syd Swasey, riding his horse, leapt across the top of this narrow section of cliff, 50 feet above the river, to win a bet. Legend also says that Butch Cassidy escaped a posse by jumping this. Another version says it was Syd Swasey who escaped the posse.

Swasey's Leap marks the beginning of 1.5 miles of short, steep Class 4 boulder drops. The first few are probably the hardest. Above 400 cfs some drops are difficult to stop above and so must be run blind. There are large pools between rapids but the sheer walls don't allow getting out on the sides. Rescues must be done from another boat.

The Black Box makes two big loops and then opens up as the rock layers start tilting down. The river flows smoothly past some sulfur springs, then cuts through the San Rafael Reef in a wider but beautiful canyon. It then runs through the flat desert and past the take-out at Black Dragon Wash or another mile farther at I-70 milepost 145, moving gently just like it starts, giving no inkling of the fury contained in the Black Boxes or the indescribable beauty of its canyons.

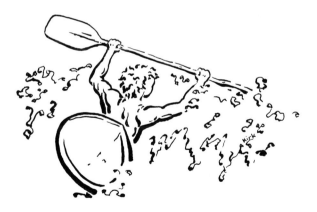

Steep, narrow drops, gigantic boulders, and overhanging cliffs make the first Black Box of the San Rafael River one of the most difficult and dangerous sections of river in Utah.

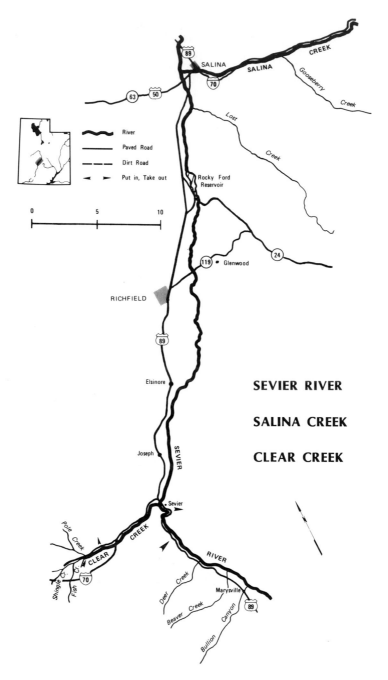

SEVIER RIVER

SALINA CREEK

CLEAR CREEK

Sevier River

Difficulty: Class 1 to 3. Most of the river is flat, but a couple of sections have whitewater up to Class 3.

Length: US-89 follows the river so runs can be any length desired.

Time of Year: Dam-controlled. Highest water is usually in May.

Average Gradient: 60 ft./mi. in the canyon below Big Rock Candy Mountain.

Flow Levels: A gage is located 1 mile south of Sevier on the right bank. The average peak is about 700 cfs, with a record of 2500 cfs on 3 June 1983.

Topo Maps: Marysville, Sevier.

Access: US-89 follows the river.

First Run: Below Big Rock Candy Mountain—Cal Giddings, Ernie Partridge, Jim Byrne, and Dick Snyder, 24 May 1969.

The Sevier is mainly flat and meandering, going through much open farm and grazing land. Several miles below Panguitch, the river goes into a canyon, picks up speed, and has a few Class 1 and 2 rapids. This is about a 6- to 10-mile run depending on where you put in and take out and is enjoyable in a canoe. It's easiest to put in at about milepost 147 and take out on the bend just after milepost 155 or at the small dam at about milepost 157.

The most exciting boating is just below Big Rock Candy Mountain. The road follows the river which facilitates scouting. A diversion dam (usually runnable) is easily seen from the road just above milepost 188. After a bridge at milepost 190, the river goes away from the road for a short distance and turns right. Where the river and canyon make a major turn left, the most difficult rapid starts (Class 3). The gage is just below here. Normal peak flows and the best boating are at about 3.0 feet, though it can be run much lower. Take out before or at the next bridge, as beyond here is a low bridge and more farmland.

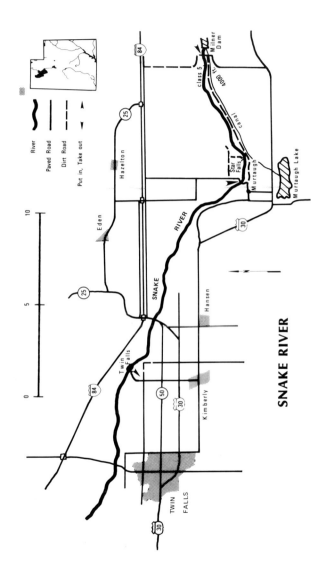

SNAKE RIVER

Snake River

Difficulty: Class 3 to 5. Steep drops, huge waves, holes.

Length: Bridge below Milner Dam to Star Falls, 7 miles; 1.3 miles more to Murtaugh Bridge; 10 more miles to Hansen Bridge; 2 more miles to last rapid; 1.3 miles more to take-out.

Time of Year: Usually April and May and September and October when farmers are not irrigating.

Average Gradient: Milner section, 24 ft./mi. (steepest drop is 80 ft./mi); Murtaugh section, 27 ft./mi.

Flow Levels: Dam-controlled. The normal high is around 17,000 cfs with a record high of 40,000 cfs on 21 June 1918. Best levels are 6,000 to 16,000 cfs.

Topo Maps: Milner Butte, Milner, Murtaugh, Eden, Kimberly, Twin Falls.

Access: Bridge below Milner Dam; dirt road to Star Falls; Murtaugh Bridge; Twin Falls Reservoir. These small roads are reached from I-84 or US-30.

First Run: Milner Section—Bryan Seeholzer, Graham Stork, Rick Hoffman, and Bruce Ring, 17 April 1982. Murtaugh section—?

MILNER DAM TO TWIN FALLS, IDAHO

The Milner section, from the dam to Star Falls, is about 9 miles long and starts right off with the hard stuff. It's all over after that except for a few little rapids and lots of flat water.

In low water, the first 2 miles have a number of separate rapids with one 15-foot ledge. In high water this turns into one long rapid with a big hole all the way across the river where a 15-foot ledge is buried—a Class 5 rapid. Below this about a mile, the river becomes mostly flat until Star Falls. A road comes in there, making it a possible put-in or take-out. The road is four-wheel-drive for a short section as it drops to the river. Most people drive to the rim then carry their boats down.

In high water you might not notice Star Falls until it's too late. Some Class 2 to 3 rapids lead into it and their noise covers the roar of the falls. The waterfall is right after a sharp right turn where the river drops about 15 feet into a huge hole and then about 25 feet over the main falls. Blundering into this would almost certainly mean death.

Amnesia and Basalt Falls are two excellent rapids between Star Falls and the Murtaugh Bridge, the most popular put-in. From here down are many Class 3 to 4 big-water rapids. At higher flows (above 9,000 cfs) the waves are huge but usually straightforward. In very low flows (can be run down to about 1800 cfs) the drops become steeper and

Dave Hildebrand punches his way through the steepest drop in the Milner section of the Snake River. Lane Johnson.

more technical, a few large holes at every level. A mile or two above Hansen Bridge is a rapid called Junkyard (the reason for the name is obvious if you look at trash on the side). Below this is Horseshoe Rapid and then the longest rapid, called Sine Waves.

Paradise Rapid is just upstream from the Hansen Bridge where two islands block the center. Go to the left side and scout the center chute. This rapid is often portaged, either from the far left or more often from the left island. It's almost always portaged above 16,000 cfs. On the far right side a waterfall dropping into a hole is a killer at all levels.

Below the Hansen Bridge the river spreads and has a ledge (called the Hooker) all the way across the river. Several chutes go through but it's hard to scout, so most boaters, at least the first time, run the far right side. Below this is Fantasy Island. You may want to land here and scout the rapid below called Let's Make a Deal, a rapid with four basalt islands dividing the river into five slots. Your choice here may have more dire consequences than on the television game show. Since your life may be at stake, I'll give you a hint: Don't choose door number 4 or 5. (Number 1 is on the left and 5 is on the right). At low flows this rapid becomes very shallow.

After another two rapids, Redshank and Duckblind, you come to the last rapid, The Idaho Connection. This has the finest surfing waves on the whole run. The lake behind Twin Falls backs up to here, 1.5 miles of paddling on the lake bringing you to the take-out on the left.

Spanish Fork River

Difficulty: Class 1 to 3. Narrow, rocks, diversions.
Length: 3.3 miles from the small UP&L dam to the Spanish Oaks Golf Course.
Time of Year: May, June.
Average Gradient: 46 ft./mi.
Flow Levels: Normal high is around 900 to 1,000 cfs with a record of 5,000 cfs on 15 May 1984. The gage is on the right 2.8 miles below Diamond Fork.
Topo Maps: Spanish Fork Peak.
Access: US-6.
First Run: Diamond Fork to UP&L dam—Cal Giddings, Gary Haltmayer, and Bill Parsinelli, 15 June 1968; below dam—Lane Johnson and Gary Nichols, 22 June 1984. (It has probably been run previously.)

Spanish Fork River was radically altered in the spring of 1983 when half the mountain on the south side of Thistle slid into the canyon and dammed the river. Unfortunately, it buried the best whitewater section. It also created a lake that was later drained, leaving an ugly mudhole. Flooding and construction of a new highway and railroad have altered the river below the slide area as well. There is still some fine boating with a few good rapids, but the best area is now between the small power plant and where the river drops through the bench just below the mouth of the canyon.

The put-in is a couple of miles above the mouth of the canyon where a short dirt road cuts off to the right to a dam. There are many Class 1 and 2 rapids, the biggest being in a straight, narrow stretch just above the canyon mouth. Even though the road is close by, you won't see much of the river from the road because a steep bank and trees block the view. This narrow part opens up at the mouth of the canyon. You'll have to portage around a diversion dam shortly after the canyon opens. It can be seen from the road.

About a quarter mile below the dam is a stone wall along the bank. Here the river goes into a canyon again and cuts through the bench. This section contains many excellent Class 2 rapids, some boulders to dodge, and a diversion dam in about a half mile. I ran the left side, but scout first. Immediately after this, the river drops through some boulders (Class 2+). It's not too much farther to where the road from the Little Acorn Restaurant crosses the river to the Spanish Oaks Golf Course, a good place to take out. The river looks easier below here.

Strawberry River

Difficulty: Class 1 to 5. Small, rocky, trees, low bridges, fairly far from help in spots. Upper part probably too tight for rafts.

Length: 21 miles from Soldier Creek Dam to Red Creek (Currant Creek); 4 miles more to bridge; 11.5 more to Starvation Reservoir.

Time of Year: Usually June.

Average Gradient: 64 ft./mi. to Red Creek (the 5.5 miles within this section from Willow Creek to Beaver Canyon drops 100 ft./mi.); below Red Creek the drop is about 22 ft./mi.

Flow Levels: Dam-controlled. Presently, the enlarged Strawberry Reservoir behind Soldier Creek Dam is being filled, and 200 cfs is all that's being released. What the flow will be once the reservoir is full is unknown. Several side streams come in below the dam increasing the flow significantly during spring. Record high was 1,020 cfs on 4 May 1952.

Topo Maps: Strawberry Reservoir NE & SE, Strawberry Peak, Deep Creek, Fruitland, Avintaquin Canyon, Strawberry Pinnacles, Sams Canyon, Rabbit Gulch.

Access: Side roads off US-40.

First Run: Lane Johnson and Gary Nichols, 25 June 1983.

For about 8 miles below the dam, the Strawberry River runs in a beautiful, narrow, mountain canyon that seldom sees visitors. Even fishermen rarely venture more than a mile below the dam. No roads go all the way through here, and the only trail ends about 3 miles below the dam near Willow Creek Canyon.

The river flows past small meadows and over beaver dams and splashes occasionally against rocks, with the hardest sections for the first 2 miles being Class 2. Then the river starts picking up. Near the confluence with Willow Creek, the gradient increases and the character of the river changes dramatically. Steep, narrow boulder drops replace the riffles. The trail ends here, and it's your last chance to turn back.

From here down the difficulty increases, with rockier, Class 3 water and some Class 4 rapids, at least one being 4+. The many sharp turns on this run make it hard to see what's ahead, and scouting often means going from eddy to eddy and always keeping a quick landing spot in sight—a serious business, but also a really fun way to run a river. Logs also block the river in places, and portages are difficult because of the thick bushes and the steep, narrow canyon. All the drops below Willow Creek can be run if they are free of trees. Watch out for some that may have hidden logs.

Neil Kahn makes one of the first runs through Pinball Rapid on Salina Creek.
Gary Nichols.

Mark White plows through the last drop of Scrambled-Egg Bend during a low water run of this most difficult stretch of the Weber River. Gary Nichols.

John Johnson demonstrates how Submarine Drop in the first Black Box of the San Rafael River was named. Jeff Niermeyer.

John Armstrong makes Paradise Rapid on the Murtaugh section of the Snake River look easy. Julie Fife.

The Yellowstone River, a jewel in the Uinta Mountains' south slope. Gary Nichols.

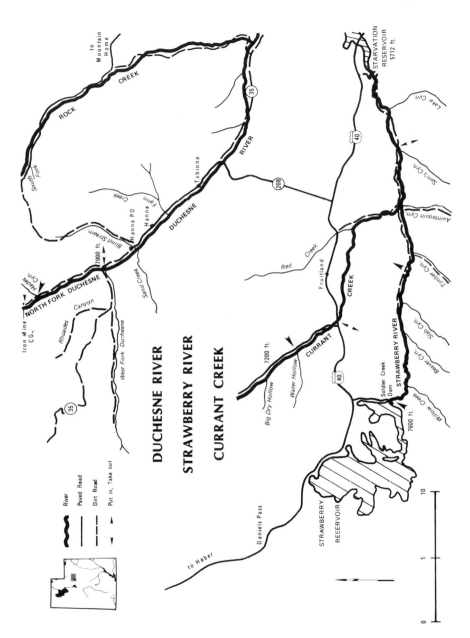

DUCHESNE RIVER

STRAWBERRY RIVER

CURRANT CREEK

After about 5 miles, the canyon opens some and the river eases a little, with longer straight stretches where you can make better time. Once you get to the dirt road, watch out for barbed-wire fences and low bridges. You're entering a summer home area. Soon the canyon opens more and the river levels out for a mile or two and then drops faster again. Most of this section can be scouted from the dirt road. The land through here is private property, so be polite and avoid getting out as much as possible.

Near Timber Canyon the scenery changes from an alpine canyon to desert cliffs. The unique Strawberry Pinnacles tower near where Red Creek (Currant Creek) comes in.

After Red Creek enters, the river is wider and straighter, and the fences and logs aren't such a problem. The best boating ends where the road crosses the river about 4 miles down from the Red Creek confluence. This is a good take-out. Several drops, some from diversions, occur about a half mile above the bridge. From the bridge to Starvation Reservoir is about 11 more miles and is slower and relatively smooth, a fairly easy stretch for canoeing.

Uinta River

Difficulty: Class 1 to 3. Rocky, trees, diversions.
Length: Uinta Valley Campground to bridge, 3.2 miles; 5.2 miles more
to the next bridge by the power plant.
Time of Year: Late May, early June.
Average Gradient: 85 ft./mi.
Flow Levels: Normal high is 1,200 to 1,500 cfs with a record of 5,000
cfs on 11 June 1965. The gage is 1,000 feet downstream from the
power plant on the left.
Topo Maps: Bollie Lake, Heller Lake, Pole Creek Cave, Whiterocks.
Access: Dirt roads off US-40 near Roosevelt.
First Run: Several sections by Les Jones (accompanied on one section
by George Jones), 29 July 1971, 21 June 1973, and June 1974.

This is one of the largest rivers coming out of the Uintas and seems to
run off slightly earlier than the rest. I've only run small sections because
it's been so low when I've gone there. From what I've looked at and the
little I've run, it's a typical Uinta River: mostly Class 2 with a few
slightly harder sections. Expect a number of logjams and areas where
the river splits into smaller channels.

The best run is an 8-mile stretch from the Uinta Valley Campground, just above Clover Creek, to the Uinta Power Plant. It's about 3
miles from the put-in to where the road crosses the river. About halfway
through this stretch is a dam that diverts water into the Power Plant
Canal. It's another 5 miles from the bridge to the power plant, with
three or four canals draining most of the water below the power plant.

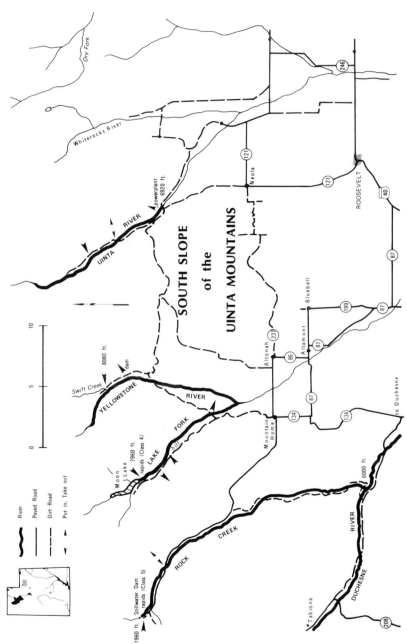

SOUTH SLOPE
of the
UINTA MOUNTAINS

Virgin River

Difficulty: North Fork, Class 3 to 5; Virgin to LaVerkin, Class 2 to 6; Virgin River Gorge, Class 1 to 3. Rocky, steep in spots, some trees. First two sections probably too tight for rafts.

Length: The road follows the North Fork, making the run whatever length you want. Virgin to LaVerkin, 7 miles; LaVerkin to the Hurricane Bridge, 12 miles; Bloomington to freeway bridge, 13 miles; 15 miles more to mouth of canyon; 5 miles more to bridge by Littlefield.

Time of Year: March through May or early June; may not be runnable in dry years.

Average Gradient: North Fork, 100 ft./mi. (steeper in spots); Virgin to LaVerkin, 62 ft./mi. (80 ft./mi. in the 4 miles of canyon); La-Verkin to Hurricane Bridge, 25 ft./mi.; Virgin River Gorge, 30 ft./mi.

Flow Levels: Normal high on the St. George gage is 700 to 1,000 cfs. Records—North Fork, 9,150 cfs on 6 December 1966; Hurricane Bridge gage, 18,700 cfs on 5 March 1978; St. George gage (started using in late 1978), 10,000 cfs on 15 February 1980; Littlefield gage, 35,200 cfs on 6 December 1966.

Topo Maps: Zion National Park, LaVerkin 4 NW, Hurricane, St. George, Purgatory Canyon, Littlefield.

First Run: North Fork—Kirk Nichols and Jim Siepman, May 1979. A section higher up including the Virgin Narrows was boated and walked by Les Jones, Cal Giddings, Bill Staude, J. and John Dewell, and Jim Byrne, 25-26 May 1975. Rest of Virgin—?

NORTH FORK

The North Fork is small, steep, and rocky through much of Zion National Park. It's fast and technical, with great logjam potential, so scout it first (scouting can mostly be done from the road). Unfortunately, depending on who the park superintendent is, you may or may not be permitted to run it. I was allowed to several years ago. The next superintendent didn't allow it, but the most recent one has allowed river running. It may be wise to write before you go: Superintendent, Zion National Park, Springdale, Utah 84767; phone (801) 772-3256.

Most of the year the Virgin is too low to run. April, May, and sometimes early June are the best months. Peak level would probably make this extremely difficult, and low water isn't much more than a trickle.

Below a few rocky drops at the end of the road, the river becomes smooth until the Court of the Patriarchs. From here to the Watchman

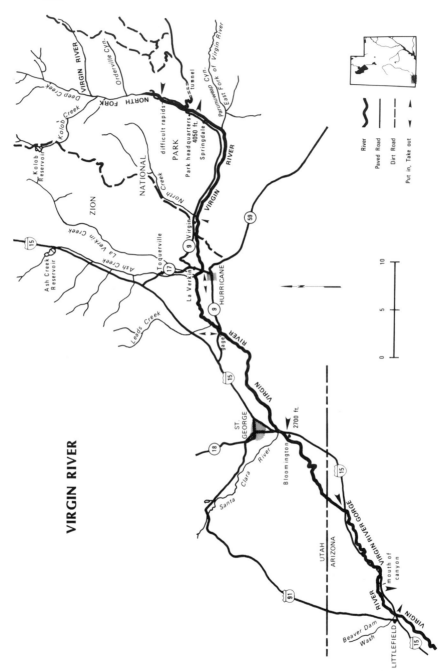

VIRGIN RIVER

Campground is the most demanding section. Put in below the diversion dam—but only if you've scouted carefully. The first quarter mile is Class 4 and 5, with some tricky drops that can give you reverse pop-ups that throw you off course.

In May 1980, a huge, partially submerged log blocked the whole river about a quarter of a mile below the Court of the Patriarchs turnoff. It was almost impossible to see from river level in time to avoid it. I lived to tell about it because I scouted first; it wasn't there the year before.

Below here the river eases to Class 3 and 3+. Just before the road crosses to the right side of the river is a diversion dam, the right runnable at our level. The river eases up a little more after this. Farther down is another dam that is too shallow and rocky to run at most levels. Soon you go under a bridge and then come to the South Campground on the right just above the bridge to Watchman Campground. The river still looks good below here.

VIRGIN TO LAVERKIN (IN MEMORIAM)

I'm glad I got to run this stretch. It was one of the outstanding advanced runs in the state. But thanks to the Quail Creek Project, it's now buried in a pipe. And the death of this section may mean the end to river running on all sections below.

What was this run like? If you put in just above the town of Virgin, the first 2 miles were Class 1. Then you dropped into a new rock layer where the river funneled through a steep, narrow, Class 3 drop into the beginning of the canyon. There were several Class 2 and 3 rapids through the next 1.5 miles. The river then cut through another new layer of rock, creating a Class 5 entrance to a narrow, vertical canyon of wall-to-wall water. Then an old diversion dam marked the beginning of a mile of boulder-filled Class 3 through Class 6 rapids until just before the mouth of the canyon, where it eased as it passed Pah Tempe Hot Springs. A hot soak here was a much welcome respite from a hard day of boating. But all this is gone and even the hot springs is threatened with destruction.

LAVERKIN TO BRIDGE BETWEEN HURRICANE AND I-15

This section starts at the hot springs and, though it isn't in a pipe, it will be mostly dry since the water is diverted through the pipe to a man-made lake. If it ever does have water, it's an enjoyable run that's fairly easy but with a fast current and enough whitewater to keep you on your toes. The gage is at the take-out bridge. You'll need a minimum of about 2.7 ft. on the gage to run this, about 400 cfs.

VIRGIN RIVER GORGE

This is the most popular section of the Virgin for boating. It has some challenging drops, numerous sand waves, and unique scenery. Hopefully it will still be runnable in spite of the damage done upstream. The new lake should drain back above this stretch; however, controlled flows may not be high enough for river running.

Put in either at Bloomington or at the I-15 bridge just past Arizona milepost 23 (westbound). It takes 2 to 3 hours from this put-in to the freeway rest stop, a couple of hours longer from Bloomington. If you aren't familiar with sand waves, you're in for a nice surprise. The shifting sandy bottom creates them, building up and disappearing and shifting around. One minute you can be surfing nicely on a wave and suddenly you're sitting in calm water.

From Bloomington to the bridge at Arizona milepost 23 is primarily Class 1. As you leave Bloomington, the river goes through a broad, open valley, but you soon wind your way into a beautiful, deep canyon. There is a barbed-wire fence across the river a short distance after the entrance to the narrow canyon. Just before you get to the bridge at I-15 milepost 23, a couple of rocky steep drops liven things up.

From the bridge, there are many rocky drops (Class 1+ to 3) until you come to the freeway rest stop. This is a good place to pull out for lunch, since there are restrooms and drinking water.

Below the rest stop the canyon narrows and the rapids get better, a few Class 3 rapids with one 3+. After you go under the freeway and make a sharp left, you come to the nasty-looking Class 3+ drop. It's at the end of a Class 2 rapid, short but steep and worth a quick scout. You go under the freeway again right after the drop.

Just above the mouth of the canyon, several warm springs enter. A couple of the best rapids follow this (Class 3 to 3+). There is a BLM take-out on the left after these rapids. The river then swings away from the highway until the next bridge about 3 miles away. Some of the best sand waves are in this section. Just below the bridge, on the left, is an interesting mineral spring with many large, yellow-and-black striped snakes. It takes 2 to 3 hours (longer in a raft) from the rest stop to the mouth of the canyon, and another hour to the bridge.

Weber River

Difficulty: Mostly Class 1 to 2, but some Class 3 to 5. Trees, rocks, diversions. Much of the river above Oakley is probably too tight for a raft.

Length: 18 miles from Holiday Park to mouth of canyon above Oakley; 11 miles more to Rockport Reservoir; 11 more to Echo Reservoir; 9.5 more to the west Henefer exit; 4.6 more to Taggart; 12 more to Morgan; 14.5 more to freeway rest stop; 3.2 more to US-89.

Time of Year: Above Rockport, June; below Echo, May to September.

Average Gradient: Above Oakley, 75 ft./mi.; Oakley to Rockport, 50 ft./mi.; Rockport to Echo, 29 ft./mi.; Echo to west Henefer exit, 19 ft./mi.; Henefer to Taggart, 22 ft./mi.; Taggart to rest stop, 15 ft./mi.; Scrambled-Egg Bend to US-89, 75 ft./mi.

Flow Levels: Above Oakley, normal high is about 1,500 cfs with a record high of 4,170 cfs on 13 June 1921. On the Gateway gage near the mouth of Weber Canyon, normal high is about 2,000 cfs with a record of 7,980 cfs on 31 May 1896.

Topo Maps: Slader Basin, Hidden Lake, Hoyt's Peak, Kamas, Crandall Canyon, Wanship, Coalville, Henefer, Devil's Slide, Morgan, Peterson, Snow Basin, Ogden.

Access: Paved and dirt road out of Oakley, US-189, I-80, I-84, US-89.

First Run: Most parts—Les Jones, 1970s.

HOLIDAY PARK TO ROCKPORT RESERVOIR

This is a very beautiful stretch, running mostly through a canyon and then through farmland. Unfortunately, everyone else thinks so too, and the entire canyon is packed with cabins and summer homes. Almost all the land is private property, so be careful where you put in and take out.

The road mainly follows the river. The pavement ends at the Smith-Morehouse junction; drive straight through the big gate, and you will come to Holiday Park after about 7 miles.

The river starts out small, rocky, and swift—mostly Class 2 with some Class 3. Watch out for low bridges and logs. About a mile below Holiday Park the river enters a large, open meadow area. It is smooth through here but splits up several times. As you come to the next bridge, the river gets rougher again for a short ways, then becomes easy and again goes through open meadows.

A half mile or so upstream from the turnoff to Smith-Morehouse Reservoir, the Weber becomes steeper and narrower and the channel splits several times. The bank becomes heavily wooded, creating great logjam danger. Some permanent-looking logjams block the whole river

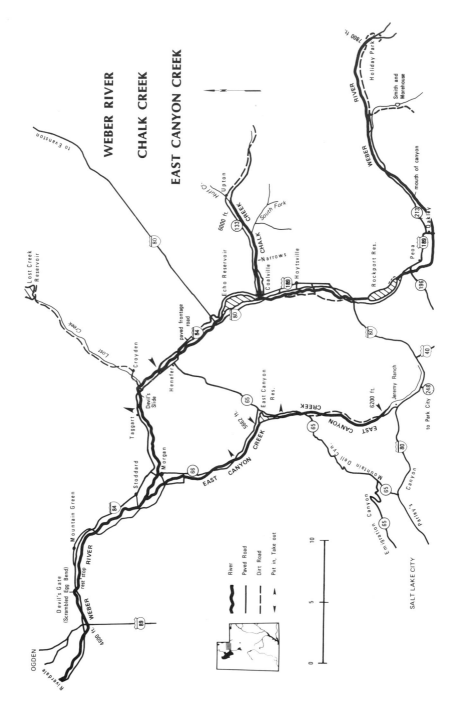

WEBER RIVER

CHALK CREEK

EAST CANYON CREEK

to Evanston

Lost Creek
Reservoir

80

Lost Creek

Croyden

Henefer

paved frontage
road

84

Devil's
Slide

Taggart

Stoddard

Morgan

66

Mountain Green

84

WEBER RIVER

rest stop

Devil's Gate
(Scrambled Egg Bend)

4800 ft.

89

OGDEN

Riverdale

EAST CANYON CREEK

5582 ft.

65

Echo Reservoir

80

80

Upton

Huff C.

6000 ft.

133

CHALK CREEK

South Fork

Narrows

Coalville

Hoytsville

189

East Canyon
Res.

65

6200 ft.

Jeremy Ranch

EAST CANYON CREEK

65

Mountain Dell Cyn.

80

65

Canyon

Parley's

Emigration Canyon

65

SALT LAKE CITY

7800 ft.

Holiday Park

Smith and
Morehouse

WEBER RIVER

mouth of canyon

213

Oakley

189

Peoa

Rockport Res.

196

80

40

248

to Park City

River
Paved Road
Dirt Road
Put in, Take out

0   5   10

but back up the water so that it's possible to drop off "spillways" created by the logs.

Scout any tight turns. Several force you through narrow slots not much wider than a kayak. Always be on the lookout for places to land quickly if the need arises. It probably will.

After the next bridge the worst is probably over, but watch out for a barbed-wire fence. The river becomes more open, and the stream from Smith-Morehouse Reservoir adds a lot of water. Don't relax too much. Some narrow, tight turns are still to come.

The river soon goes under the main road. Watch out for fallen cottonwood trees below here. About a quarter mile above the mouth of the canyon is a gage. Some good surfing waves are here, and shortly below is a good take-out at a short turnout from the road just before you go up a hill as you're leaving the canyon.

Below this access spot, the river looks like it goes into a dam. It really doesn't. The river goes left and what you see are the headgates for a canal. However, a dam about a mile below here should be portaged. In another half mile is a much larger dam with about a 15-foot drop onto cement. Portage to the left. This is where water is diverted from the Weber River to the Provo River.

Especially at high water, the section out in the valley to Rockport Reservoir is very enjoyable with lots of waves and fast water. There is a fair amount of maneuvering around logs, so watch out. Above the main road through Oakley (US-189), the river breaks into many channels for a short ways, no channel being very big. After the US-189 bridge, the river is more open and has fewer logjams. About a mile below this is a low bridge that you'll have to walk around. Watch for logs below here. Just before coming to the west hillside there is a cement wall and a drop off a dam. It was runnable and great surfing at 1400 cfs.

The scenery changes when you get to the hills to the west. For about a mile there are cliffs and steep hills on the left that make it quite pretty. The waves can be big and rolling through here. A bridge for U-196 (Brown's Canyon Road) crosses the river, and right after it is a rocky dam that is easiest to run on the right. The next bridge has a really nice surfing wave below it. You may want to get out here because you're not allowed to park anywhere near the next bridge—which is right at the reservoir and lets you into the state park. A fee is charged to enter the state park.

ROCKPORT RESERVOIR TO ECHO RESERVOIR

The full run (putting in just below the dam at Rockport and getting out at the Coalville exit on I-80) is about 12 miles, with a shuttle of about 10 miles by way of the backroad or the freeway. Four other roads cross the river between Rockport and Coalville, all of which are good access points. Plan on three to four hours of boating time, and about ten portages as well.

The run is mainly through pretty farmland. However, in several sections, if you're not careful, you might find yourself in the driver's seat of an abandoned car. These old cars are really the only things marring the view of cottonwoods, willows, and foothills.

Many obstacles on this run make it less enjoyable and more dangerous than many. Before you've even made it through the first mile, you'll be confronted by two barbed-wire fences and at least one logjam. Right after the road from Wanship crosses the river you will need to portage the first large diversion dam—unless the river is high. After this the portages are farther apart. Plan on at least three more barbed-wire fences, two more diversion dams, many logjams you can barely maneuver around, several trees all the way across the river, and an untold number of overhanging bushes, many of which have sharp thorns.

If you're still interested in boating this section, I'd recommend that your first run be at relatively low water. Highest water is usually in June, but since the Weber is dam-controlled, it varies depending on irrigation needs. It's often runnable in August and early September.

ECHO THROUGH HENEFER

Watch out for a fence or two in this section; an occasional log also creates problems. A number of small falls (diversion dams) are scattered through here, and some are rocky. A couple of people have drowned going over in innertubes when caught in the backwash. I've never had any trouble in a canoe or kayak as long as I kept the boat straight and not sideways.

Through this 10-mile run, the river winds past cottonwood trees and open farmland. It's a picturesque run until you come to the many junk cars dumped along the banks before Henefer.

The paved frontage road between Henefer and Echo is the best road to take if you're doing a bicycle shuttle. There is also a dirt road that follows the river more closely, giving access to a couple of easy rock gardens. Most of the run is Class 1 with the drops and rocky areas being Class 2.

HENEFER TO TAGGART

This 5-mile stretch is the most popular kayak run on the Weber. Easy access to the river is found at the west Henefer exit. About a quarter mile below here you enter a Class 2 rock garden that lasts almost a mile. A number of inexperienced canoeists have destroyed their boats here, so be careful.

After the rock garden and just before the bridges at the Croyden exit are some waves. In high water, watch out for the bridge just below them. You may have to get out and walk around it because there's so little clearance.

Just below the bridge is a good access point to the river from the Croyden road. About a half mile below here, beyond a freeway bridge, is another rock garden that goes past Devil's Slide, the site of an annual slalom race. Following this are occasional drops where you can surf in a canoe or kayak and do some shallow pop-ups.

At one point the river goes under the freeway through a slalom course of concrete pillars. Just right of center is a fairly straight slot through the pillars. The waves through here and the pillars team up to make an interesting 100-yard section.

Just above the Taggart exit from the freeway is a railroad bridge crossing the river. Get out here unless you're ready to run Taggart Falls (Class 2+). This is usually run on the left. Except at low levels, the water recirculates strongly after the falls and will definitely hold a boat going over sideways. A couple of boaters have almost drowned here in high water.

TAGGART TO REST STOP BELOW MOUNTAIN GREEN

This is a long, seldom-run section (26.5 miles). Plan on taking a full day for the run—longer if irrigation has taken most of the water. There are a couple of easy rapids at first, then you encounter several diversion dams. Some can be run, while others have 4- to 8-foot drops onto cement.

It's about 12 miles to Morgan. A large dam near here diverts half the river for irrigation during the summer. It's possible to get out here if you want to avoid the slow and shallow section to Peterson. Watch out for barbed-wire fences if you do continue on.

From Peterson on down is fairly slow and easy. A couple of drops can be run in higher water. Again, watch out for fallen trees. Just below the Mountain Green exit where the river goes under a railroad bridge is a nice little rapid. Below here the river slows down as it backs up behind the dam just below the freeway rest stop. During most of the summer, what's left of the river is almost entirely diverted at this dam. Often only a trickle is left in the main channel until after the power plant.

SCRAMBLED-EGG BEND (DEVIL'S GATE)
TO MOUTH OF CANYON

About a quarter mile below the dam, the water begins to pick up speed. It really starts dropping, and as the river turns right it funnels into a narrow channel at the head of a long horseshoe bend. There's a cliff on the left and a concrete wall on the right supporting the old highway. In high water expect some big waves and holes. The river then cuts sharply

Finesse and good river reading skills allow Mark White to dodge the many jagged rocks at Scrambled-Egg Bend on the Weber River. Gary Nichols.

left, widens a little, and makes its steepest drop through many sharp boulders.

Always scout Scrambled-Egg Bend very carefully. It's a dangerous section (Class 5 at high water) because of the shallowness of the water, the speed of the river, and the sharpness of the rocks. If you run it, don't tip over or you'll get banged up and probably have your boat smashed. Two different rafts, each filled with 3 inexperienced river runners, have gone through here. Both rafts flipped resulting in two deaths from each party.

The bottom part of Scrambled-Egg Bend was changed in 1984, and the excavation work going on in the area will probably change it more. So far, rocks and boulders have been dumped in on both sides to keep the bank from eroding. New waves and holes have been created, increasing the difficulty of the run. This eases slightly as the river goes under the railroad bridge, but large concrete blocks bristling with rebar have recently been dumped into the river as it bends to the right, creating a series of hazards that must be scouted. After that, the river is constant Class 2 to 3 down to the power plant. Few eddies and lots of rock dodging in lower water increase the challenge here. It's a good idea to run this lower section before tackling Scrambled-Egg Bend. If you can't handle it with ease, don't try the bend.

The river slows down just before the power plant. If the gates are down, you must portage. If they're open, you should check for obstructions before running. Be aware of a short drop with recirculating water at the gates. In high water this can stop and trap a boat and boater. Usually the far right side is still runnable in high water.

After the power plant, the river gets larger because of the re-entry of water that was diverted above Scrambled-Egg Bend. Below here the water is fast with some good Class 2 to 3 rapids. Be sure you get out at the first bridge, less than a mile down. Immediately below the bridge is a large cement drop with a wicked reversal that can kill. From this falls to US-89, the river is swift but easy.

MOUTH OF WEBER CANYON (US-89) TO RIVERDALE

This is a very pretty and pleasant run. The freeway parallels the river close by, but the cottonwoods and willows screen it from view. It's about a 6-mile stretch and takes at least an hour in high water. Expect many shallow places in anything but high water. Also watch out for trees caught in the middle or hanging out on the bends.

The current is swift and there are many Class 1 rapids and a few Class 2. The river splits into several channels in a couple of spots. Where the river splits and the main channel isn't obvious, I found that all the channels were good.

You need to watch out for two drops. The first is by the Uintah turnoff. When you pass by some houses on the left bank, look for the falls about a quarter mile below. The river makes a steep drop through boulders. It's sometimes choked with trees but is runnable when clear.

The second drop (more of a riverwide reversal) is just before the Riverdale turnoff. It's easy to scout from the road. I run it, but scout and decide for yourself; it could be tricky in an open canoe. Take out just below here at the Riverdale exit.

152

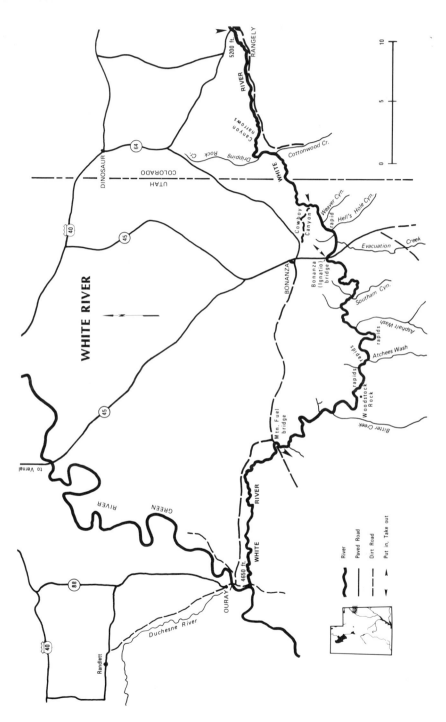

White River

Difficulty: Class 1 to 2. Mostly flat with a few easy rapids; more difficult during high water. Trees, far from help.

Length: Rangely to Bonanza Bridge, 37 miles; Cowboy Canyon to Bonanza Bridge, 7.5 miles; Bonanza Bridge to Mountain Fuel Bridge,
38 miles; Mountain Fuel Bridge to confluence with the Green
River, 20 miles.

Time of Year: Usually peaks in late May or June. This is the best time
for rafts, but it may be a bit rough for inexperienced canoeists. It
can be run most of a high-water year.

Average Gradient: Rangely to Cowboy Canyon, 6 ft./mi.; Cowboy
Canyon to Bonanza Bridge, 11 ft./mi.; Bonanza Bridge to Mountain Fuel Bridge, 7 ft./mi.; Mountain Fuel Bridge to confluence
with Green River, 2.5 ft./mi.

Flow Levels: A gage (not readable without a key) is located on the right
bank downstream from the Bonanza Bridge on U-45. Normal peak
is about 3,000 cfs, with a recorded high of 8,160 cfs on 15 July
1929. I've heard of it being run at 300 cfs, but plan on walking in
several places below 600 cfs. For flow information, call the USGS
in Vernal at (801) 789-1128, or the recorded river-flow information
(National Weather Service) number in Salt Lake City, (801)
539-1311. These give the flow at a gage near Ouray.

Topo Maps: Rangely, Banty Point, Walsh Knolls, Weaver Ridge,
Southam Canyon, Asphalt Wash, Archy Bench, Redwash SW,
Ouray SE, Ouray.

Access: Rangely, Colorado (you can put in right in town, or good dirt
roads follow down both sides of the river and get you into the
canyon); Cowboy Canyon; Bonanza Bridge (3 miles south of Bonanza; old Ignatio Bridge has been torn out); Mountain Fuel
Bridge; Ouray.

The White River starts in the Colorado Rockies. After leaving the mountains it becomes a meandering river with excellent camping among the
cottonwoods. This is one of the best beginning canoe/camping trips in
the state, but it is being continually threatened with a dam. Don't be
afraid to voice your opposition to it, if you choose to.

Fossils and petrified wood can be found in places along the river.
There are also many arches and windows in the cliffs of the canyon. The
lush river bottom provides food, water, and shelter from the hot desert,
making it a haven for beaver, wild horses, deer, golden eagles, and
Canadian geese. The biting flies will enjoy your visit; however, some

The White River, suitable for all craft, is especially ideal for canoes. Kirk Nichols.

other wildlife may not welcome you. Heavy use in the spring may destroy the incentive of nesting geese and raptors.

River trips can range from a day to a week depending on where you put in and take out. In low water, watch out for rocks. The biggest hazards usually are trees, which get hung up in shallows or stick out into the river from the banks, especially at bends.

After the bridge at Rangely, the river winds through miles of goosenecks or bowknot bends, offering you the opportunity of looking into the blank faces of many cows. A number of homes have been built through here. Once you get out of the wide valley, though, the river is straighter and the scenery more pleasant. By dirt road you can skip the meanderings and go directly to where the river enters the hills on the west side of the valley. The road on the left bank is probably the easiest to find from Rangely.

The canyon narrows about halfway to Cowboy Canyon, and from here on the scenery is prettiest. The road leaves the river here, although a few others come in farther down. A fairly good dirt road, when dry, comes in at Cowboy Canyon. The turnoff, about 1 mile east of Bonanza on C-64, is marked with a sign about 100 feet down the road. It's a little hard to see if you're not looking carefully. It's about 4 miles from the turnoff down to the river—part of which is in a wash.

About 45 minutes (4 miles) below Cowboy Canyon is a half-mile section of rapids (Class 2). The Bonanza Bridge can be a take-out for the section above or a put-in for the lower section. The road from Bo-

The Yampa River has cut one of the most beautiful canyons in Dinosaur National Monument. Kirk Nichols.

nanza to the river has been straightened and paved and a new bridge put in. In doing this, the old, historic cabins on the hill were torn down.

Below here, logs seem to be a greater hazard. The proposed damsite is also below here. Some of the best rapids (Class 2 to 2+) are in this stretch. They start just before the river reaches its most southerly point and are scattered over the next 7 miles. Some develop large waves at flows over 2,500 cfs. In a calm, straight stretch after these, if you look to the left, you can see what I call Woodstock Rock, named after the bird in the Peanuts comic strip. Shortly after is a small rapid. The river slows considerably the last 5 miles above the Mountain Fuel Bridge, and the canyon starts lowering and opening up.

The Mountain Fuel Bridge is about 18 miles west of Bonanza on the road to Ouray. The road is rough, hard-packed dirt but is easily passable in a passenger car. Signs direct you to the bridge, and although there is no sign at the actual turnoff (if coming from Bonanza), the tall cottonwood trees a hundred yards south from the junction make the take-out easily visible.

Plan on at least 6 hours of boating time (with steady paddling at about 1200 cfs) from Rangely to Cowboy Canyon, 2 hours more to the Bonanza Bridge, and another 7 or 8 hours to the Mountain Fuel Bridge. Allow more time if in a raft. From Rangely to the Mountain Fuel Bridge makes a nice 3-to-4 day trip. I'm not familiar with the section from the Mountain Fuel Bridge to Ouray but guess it would take another day (20 miles), with less spectacular scenery and slower current.

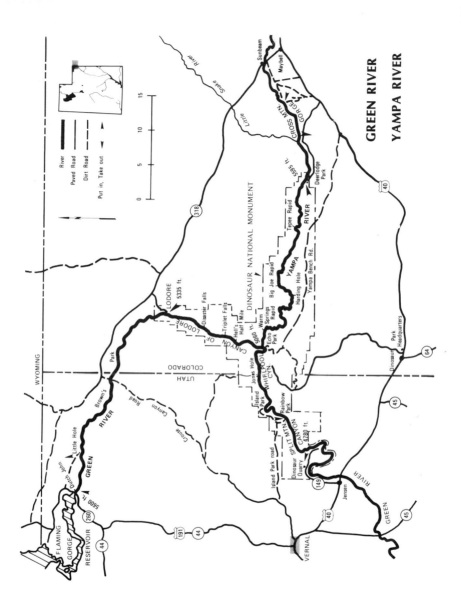

GREEN RIVER
YAMPA RIVER

Yampa River

Difficulty: Cross Mountain, Class 3 to 6, depending on water level. Rocky, tight turns, holes. Deerlodge Park to the Green River, mainly flat with a couple of Class 3 rapids and one Class 4. Big waves and holes.

Length: Cross Mountain, 3 miles; Deerlodge Park to confluence, 46 miles.

Time of Year: Highest water is in May and June—a good time for the main run. Cross Mountain is extremely hazardous in high water, but is safer in late June or July when the flow is less than 2,000 but above 500 cfs. Both sections are often too low to run after July unless there is a heavy rain.

Average Gradient: Cross Mountain, 65 ft./mi.; main run, 11 ft./mi.

Flow Level: The main run usually peaks at about 15,000 cfs, with highs around 20,000 cfs. Cross Mountain runs slightly lower because the Little Snake River enters below it. A gage at Maybell gives the flow at Cross Mountain. Call the National Weather Service river flow number in Salt Lake City for information on both stretches: (801) 539-1311.

Topo Maps: Cross Mountain—Lone Mountain, Elk Springs. Deer lodge Park to confluence—Elk Springs, Indian Water Canyon, Haystack Rock, Tanks Peak, Hell's Canyon, Canyon of Lodore South.

Access: From US-40; see each section for details.

First Run: Cross Mountain—Cal Giddings party, August 1965; Below Deerlodge Park—? Jim Baker and Sam Anderson (fur traders), sometime before 1869; Nathan and Parley Galloway, Spring 1909.

CROSS MOUNTAIN

This is by far the most difficult section of the Yampa River.

Between 500 and 2,000 cfs, the river is extremely good technical kayaking but not overly difficult, mainly Class 3 to 4. The waves aren't huge but the maneuvering is very tight through narrow slots, around giant boulders, over ledges, twisting through "S" turns—just a magnificent run in a unique canyon. At high levels (above 4,000 cfs) the difficulty approaches Class 5, with the first rapid (a Class 6 riverwide hole) portaged.

The course is only 3 miles long, cutting through the middle of the mountain, but plan on at least 2 hours to run it. You will probably want to scout many of the drops, since it's very difficult to see far ahead. The first mile has the most difficult rapids.

The road to the put-in is difficult (about Class 4 with a couple of Class 5 drops), but small passenger cars can make it down if the road is dry and if driven very carefully. Two miles east of the Deerlodge Park turnoff on US-40, turn left on Moffat County Road 85 (dirt). After two more miles the main road curves to the right. Take the straight road at a sign "Cedar Spring Draw allotment #15." After about a quarter mile, take the less-traveled road that drops to the left. The road gets rougher through here. In 2 miles the road forks. The left goes to an overlook at the entrance to Cross Mountain Gorge. The right used to go to the river but has been thoroughly gullied out. It's an easy carry down to the river, though.

If the roads are muddy, another road cuts off US-40 a couple of miles east of County Road 85 that's passable when wet. In about 5 miles you reach the river. The road then goes right and follows the river east to the town of Sunbeam and C-318. Put in just upstream of where you first meet the river and if the river is low plan on 2 hours of flat water to the canyon entrance.

The take-out is from the road to Deerlodge Park. There's a turn-out and parking area at the mouth of Cross Mountain Gorge.

Two dams proposed for the Yampa—the last free-flowing river in the entire Colorado River basin—are on hold at present, thanks to the many people who got involved and opposed them. The lower one would be at the mouth of Cross Mountain Gorge and would inundate the entire run in this wild canyon. It would also destroy high-water boating downriver in the main section.

DEERLODGE PARK TO THE CONFLUENCE
WITH THE GREEN RIVER

This is the main run on the Yampa, and several commercial companies operate here. Permits are required for private parties and are difficult to obtain. For permit information, contact: Superintendent, Dinosaur National Monument, Dinosaur, Colorado 81610; phone (303) 374-2216.

To get to the put-in, turn north off US-40 about 8 miles east of Elk Springs. The turnoff is marked. Follow the road for 14 miles to the Deerlodge put-in. Take out at Echo Park or farther down the Green River below Split Mountain, east of Jensen by the dinosaur quarry.

From Deerlodge Park, the portal to Yampa Canyon is visible. This canyon is the most scenic of those in Dinosaur National Monument, cutting through Blue Mountain, the easternmost spur of the Uintas. For 45 miles you're in this deep canyon composed mainly of Weber Sandstone and the Morgan Formation.

If you're lucky you may see some bighorn sheep. You will see hoodoos, picturesque Harding Hole, and serpentine bends below Harding Hole where you travel 7 miles to cover 2 straight miles. Castle Park and Mantle Ranch are 12 miles above the confluence. This is the only car access in Yampa Canyon, but the road runs on private property. Just below is Mantle Cave, where evidence of pre-Columbian Indians of the Fremont culture has been found. Some of the best displays of desert varnish (manganese and iron oxide stains left from water evaporating on the cliffs) can be seen at Tiger Wall.

The river is mostly smooth but fast water, several smaller rapids appearing in low water. There are three major rapids: Tepee, Big Joe, and Warm Springs. Tepee is 8 miles from the canyon entrance. Starting here and for the next 2.5 miles is one of the fastest stretches of the river. Big Joe Rapid is halfway through the canyon about 21 miles from the entrance. Warm Springs Rapid is just over 4 miles upstream from the confluence with the Green River.

Until 1965 there was no Warm Springs Rapid—only a riffle. On the night of 10 June, a flash flood in Warm Springs Draw sent tons of rock and gravel crashing into the river. The most difficult rapid in the canyon was thus formed and was later made worse by slabs of rock falling from the cliff on the left. The next day two rafts approached, unaware of what had happened, and the first boatman was killed. His passengers made it through, but he was thrown from the raft and wasn't found for 17 days.

Warm Springs Rapid is long and fairly technical. In high water the waves are large and the current draws everything toward giant holes— holes that have flipped the largest rafts. In a kayak under experienced hands, the rapid is not too difficult because of the great maneuverability of these small craft; but in a waterlogged raft, the precise maneuvering for a clean run can be difficult.

The last 4 miles are slow before the Yampa joins the Green River at Echo Park.

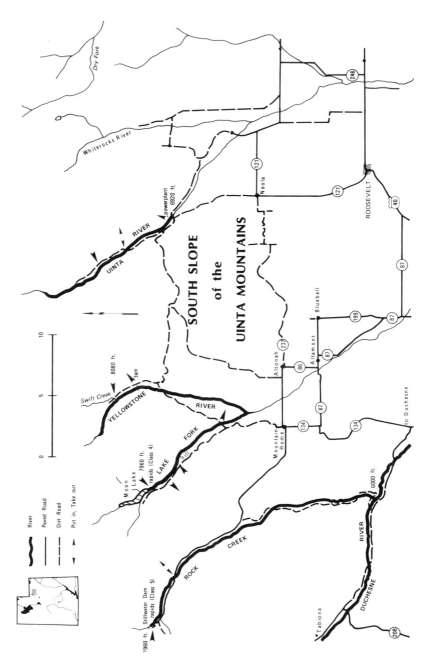

Yellowstone River

Difficulty: Class 2 to 2+. Continuous, rocky, trees.
Length: 2 miles. Other sections are possible.
Time of Year: Late May and early June.
Average Gradient: 104 ft./mi.
Flow Levels: Normal peak is around 800 cfs with a record of 2,240 cfs
    on 19 June 1983.
Topo Maps: Burnt Mill Spring.
Access: Off US-40. U-134 to Mountain Home, then dirt roads.
First Run: Les Jones, 21 June 1971.

SWIFT CREEK CAMPGROUND TO RESERVOIR CAMPGROUND

This is another heavily wooded Uinta river, so watch out for fallen
trees. It's mostly a fast, Class 2+ stretch. About three quarters of the
way through the run the river splits several times. High water and
beaver have teamed to down many trees and block all the channels for
about a hundred yards. The run ends shortly afterward on the small
reservoir.

A number of other sections are possible both above and below this.
I'm not very familiar with them, but they appear to either have more
logs across or more difficult access.

Doug Heinrich finds a perfect hole for endos in Cross Mountain Canyon of the Yampa River. Linda Gary.

Rough Divisions According to Difficulty

(AT MEDIUM FLOWS UNLESS OTHERWISE INDICATED)

Runs above intermediate level are generally too difficult for most open canoeists; also, open canoeists should figure their ability one level lower, i.e., advanced canoeists should probably stick to intermediate runs (or lower).

BEGINNER RUNS (NOT NOVICE, CLASS 1 TO 2)

Bear River—most sections not described in book.
Chalk Creek—except for "Narrows."
Colorado River—Horsethief and Ruby Canyons; Cisco to Fisher Towers; just below Big Bend to Confluence.
Dirty Devil River—the isolation makes this an advanced-beginner run.
Green River—Brown's Park; dinosaur quarry to Sand Wash; Green River to Confluence.
Jordan River—Utah Lake to the Narrows; 3900 South to Rose Park.
Provo River—Deer Creek Reservoir to first diversion dam.
San Rafael River—to San Rafael campground.
Sevier River—most areas not described.
White River—some is advanced-beginner in difficulty, especially at high water.

INTERMEDIATE (CLASS 2+ TO 3)

Bear River—Oneida Narrows.
Big and Little Cottonwood Creeks—lower half of sections in the city.
Chalk Creek—Narrows section.
Clear Creek
Colorado River—Fisher Towers to Big Bend.
Currant Creek—a couple of harder spots.
Duchesne River—almost all above town of Duchesne. Including North Fork at medium flows.
East Canyon Creek
Escalante River
Ferron Creek—lower flows.
Green River—Red Canyon (below Flaming Gorge); Desolation and Gray Canyons (advanced-intermediate); Split Mountain (advanced-intermediate).
Gunnison Gorge—low to medium flows.
Jordan River—the Narrows.
Logan River—through town.

Muddy Creek—isolation makes it advanced-intermediate.

Price River—Price to Woodside.

Provo River—Woodland section, and section below Bridal Veil Falls.

San Juan River

South Fork of Ogden River—one advanced rapid.

Spanish Fork River

Sevier River—below Big Rock Candy Mountain.

Virgin River Gorge—a couple of advanced-intermediate sections.

Weber River—all but the section from Devil's Gate to the mouth, and the section above Oakley.

ADVANCED (CLASS 4)

Bear River—Hayden and East Forks (a couple of hard sections) and down to the state line.

Big and Little Cottonwood Creeks—upper parts after entering the valley.

Black's Fork—some sections are easier.

Blacksmith Fork—lower section.

Bruneau and Jarbidge Rivers (Idaho)

Colorado River—Cataract Canyon at medium flows; Westwater Canyon.

Cottonwood Creek—low to medium flows.

Dolores River

Duchesne—North Fork in high water.

Ferron Creek—high flows.

Fremont River—below campground.

Green River—Canyon of Lodore.

Gunnison (Colorado)—Gunnison Gorge in high water.

Lake Fork—lower section.

Logan River—canyon except last two miles which are harder.

Ogden River—all but the last two miles which are harder.

Price River—Scofield Reservoir to Price Canyon; Woodside to Green River.

Provo River—Bridal Veil Falls section at medium flows.

Salina Creek—except for a couple of harder sections.

Snake River—Twin Falls section (Murtaugh).

Weber River—above Oakley and below Scrambled-Egg Bend to mouth of canyon.

Yampa River (Colorado)—much of this is intermediate.

Yellowstone River—would be intermediate except for logjams.

EXPERT (CLASS 4+ AND HARDER) (MOST ARE EXTREMELY DIFFICULT FOR A RAFT)

Bear River (Idaho)—Black Canyon.

Colorado River—Cataract Canyon at high water.

Cottonwood Creek—high water.
Fremont River—above campground.
Huntington Creek
Lake Fork—upper section.
Logan River—last two miles of canyon.
Ogden River—last two miles of canyon.
Price River—Price Canyon section.
Provo River—Bridal Veil Falls section in high water.
Rock Creek—upper.
Salina Creek—"Pinball" section.
San Rafael—both Black Box sections.
Snake River—Milner section.
Strawberry River—above Red Creek.
Virgin River—North Fork; Virgin to LaVerkin (gone).
Weber River—Scrambled-Egg Bend.
Yampa River—Cross Mountain section.

Glossary

Cartwheel—when a boat flips end over end several times.

C-1 or C-2—decked one-person or two-person canoes.

Deadfall area—an area covered with fallen trees.

Eddy—the water behind an outcropping or rock that flows upstream.

Eddyline—the swirling line between an eddy and the main current.

Endo—flipping a boat end over end by driving either end into the upstream side of a hole.

Gabion walls—rock walls with some type of screen or wire mesh holding them in place.

Hole-riding contest—a contest where boaters compete in freestyle and acrobatic events in a particular hole, performing endos, surfing, pirouettes, paddle twirling, or anything they think will impress the judges.

Hoodoo—rock formations larger on top than underneath due to a soft underlayer that erodes quicker than the capping rock, creating strange mushroom- and goblin-shaped forms.

Low-head dams—generally a small dam where the water spills freely over the top rather than being blocked and forced down a narrow spillway.

Pool-drop—where a river drops in a stairstep fashion. Rather than long continuous rapids, the river drops through a shorter rapid and then pools or slows for a while and then drops again.

Pop-up—when a boat is stood nearly vertically by a curling wave or hole; can be done either forward or backward.

Portage—carrying your boat overland.

Pour-over—a place where the water pours off the top of a ledge or dam creating a reversal or hole at the bottom.

Reversal—another name for a hole; any wave that curls back on itself.

Royalex—trademark name for several layers of tough ABS plastic laminated together with a layer of vinyl on the outside. It comes from Uniroyal in sheets that are vacuum formed into the desired canoe shape, creating a one-piece, seamless canoe.

Self-bailing raft—a raft with the floor attached in such a way as to allow water to flow through the edges.

Surfing—sliding down the face of a wave just like ocean surfing. On a river the wave stands still while the water moves by; on the ocean the opposite happens but the result is the same.

Tailrace—the end of the chute of water spilling from a dam.

Undercut spot—a rock or ledge cut deeper under the surface than on top, creating something of a cave where a boat or boater can be forced under and trapped.

Vertical pin—when a boat goes over a steep drop and the end catches under a rock or ledge, stopping the boat and trapping it in a near vertical position.